TEASE TO PLEASE!

The Erotic Art of

Adrian Velez

AGE '13

an SQP presentation

Pleased to Tease!

Artist Adrian Velez on illustrating that itch that loves to be scratched...

Age here again with my second book. When I finished work on my first book, *The Art of Adrian Velez - Age of Delights*, I was praying that it would be a success. Not just because of every artist's natural desire for their work to do well and be accepted by the unwashed masses (you know, people like YOU), but also because I had dreams of doing a follow-up book. A sequel, if you will. But not a sequel in the *Conan the Destroyer* vein - more like a *Terminator 2* kind of sequel.

Since I already gave you the history of my life in my first book, I'll fill you in on what I've done since it was released. After *Age of Delights*, many new doors opened for me and I am still grateful for all the wonderful opportunities that I received as a result. For example, I worked with acclaimed record producer Salaam Remi on drawing the cover for his latest album. It was a long and arduous process, especially since it required that I draw a man (anybody who purchased my first book knows that I primarily draw the female of the species), but I was able to come through in the end with a finished product that impressed both myself and the producer. (From what I heard, he stared at that album cover all day the first time he saw it.)

After that, I started working with a rock band called *In This Moment*. I drew their tour posters as well as the album cover for one of their singles. I also contributed to their merchandise by creating a sketch of the lead singer that they ended up putting on t-shirts that they sold during their tour in 2013. At this moment I am still working with *In This Moment* (get it?), and I hope that it's an experience that never ends.

And now a little about the book you're holding in your grubby little hands, *Tease to Please*. (Sounds like a Skinemax movie, right?) What I wanted to accomplish with my sophomore publication was to make it the best that it could be. Now you're probably asking yourself *"Isn't that what you wanted to do with your first book?,"* and the answer is *"Yes"* - but I'm always pushing myself to the limit, like Tony Montana (minus the cocaine and cocaine-addicted wife.) So what I did in this book that I didn't do in my first one was to present my models in a more realistic way. My interpretations of them in *Age of Delights* were more caricature-based compared to how they look in *Tease to Please*, where you see them more or less as they appear in real life. The best way to notice this difference is by comparing the illustrations of the models that appear in both books, such as Mistress Juliya, Metal Sanaz, and Vera Vanguard. (In case you didn't know, all of the drawings in this book - as well as in my first tome - are based on real people and not on characters that I created.)

As was the case with *Age of Delights*, I would like to send a huge "THANK YOU!" to all of my beautiful and amazing angels who appear in *Tease to Please* (eat your heart out Charlie), without whose cooperation and undying support this book would obviously not be possible. I would also like to take this moment to dedicate this book to my late father who unfortunately passed away during the making of it. He was proud of the work I did on the first one and I'm sure that he would be even prouder of what I accomplished with this one.

Last but not least, I hope that each and every person who purchases this book comes away with the feeling that *"Yes, it does get better with Age!"*

Adrian (AGE) Velez

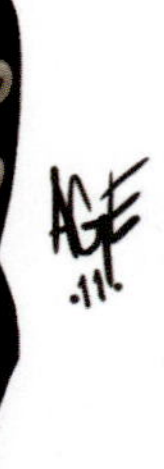

Tease to Please!
The Erotic Art of Adrian Velez

Book design by Grassy Knoll Studios.

Published by SQP Inc.
PO Box 248 - Columbus NJ 08022

Sal Quartuccio & Bob Keenan - Publishers

For a free, full color catalog a showcasing the entire SQP line of erotic, fantasy, and pin-up artwork, go to:
www.sqpartbooks.com

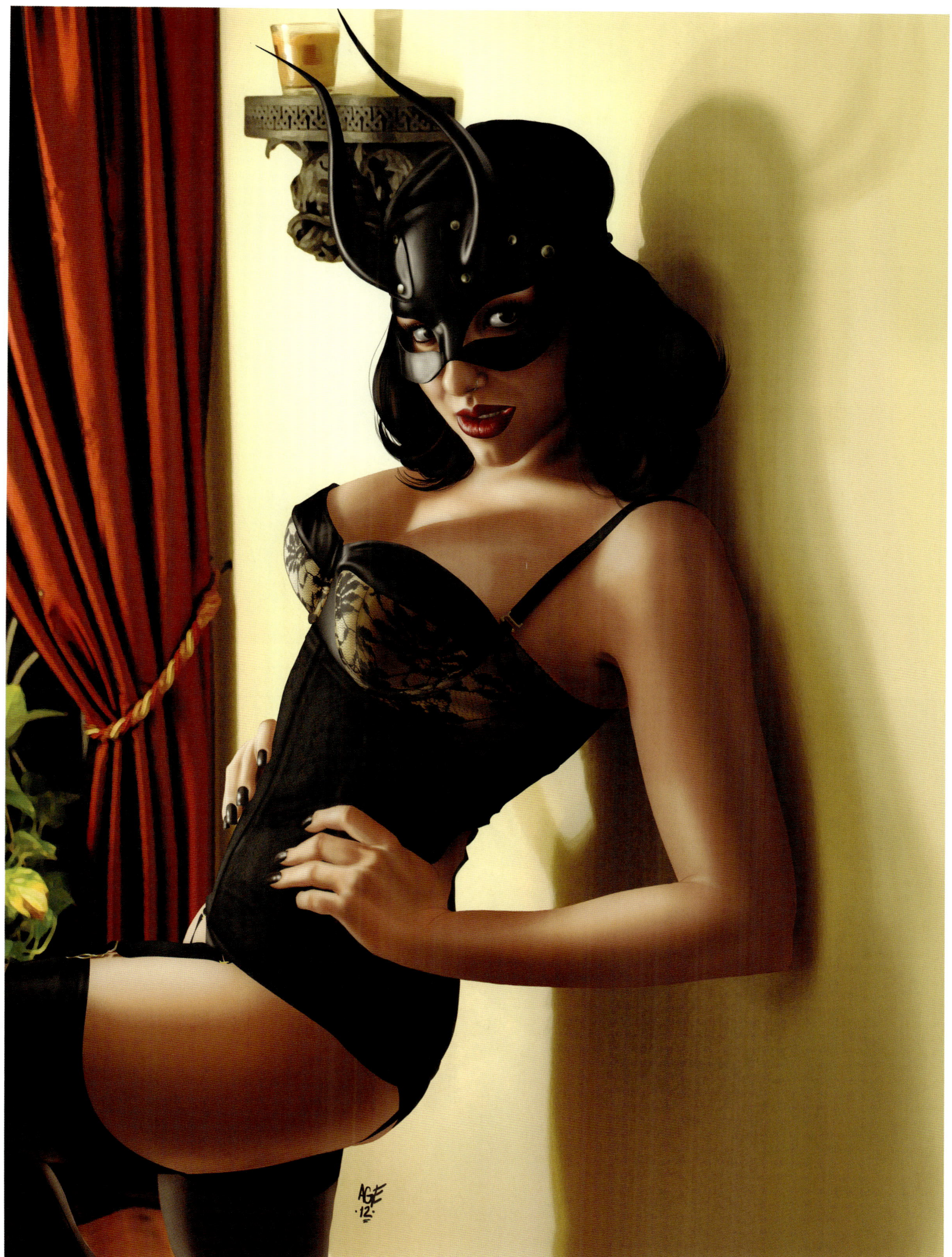

Devil Mask

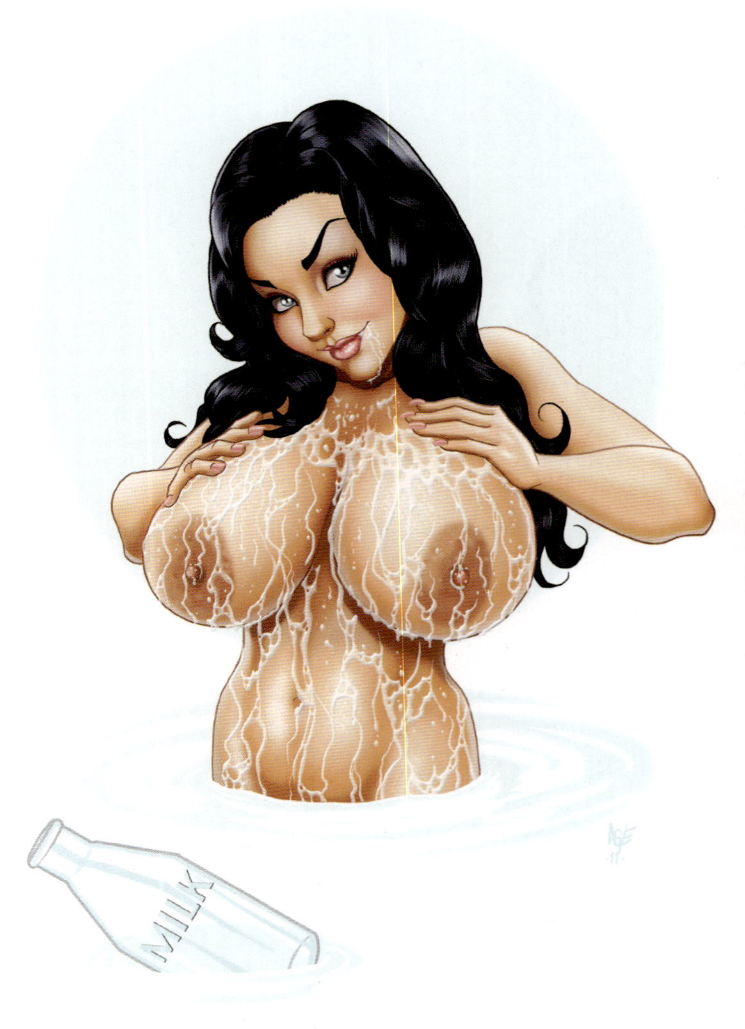

Lusty n' Busty Milky Vicky

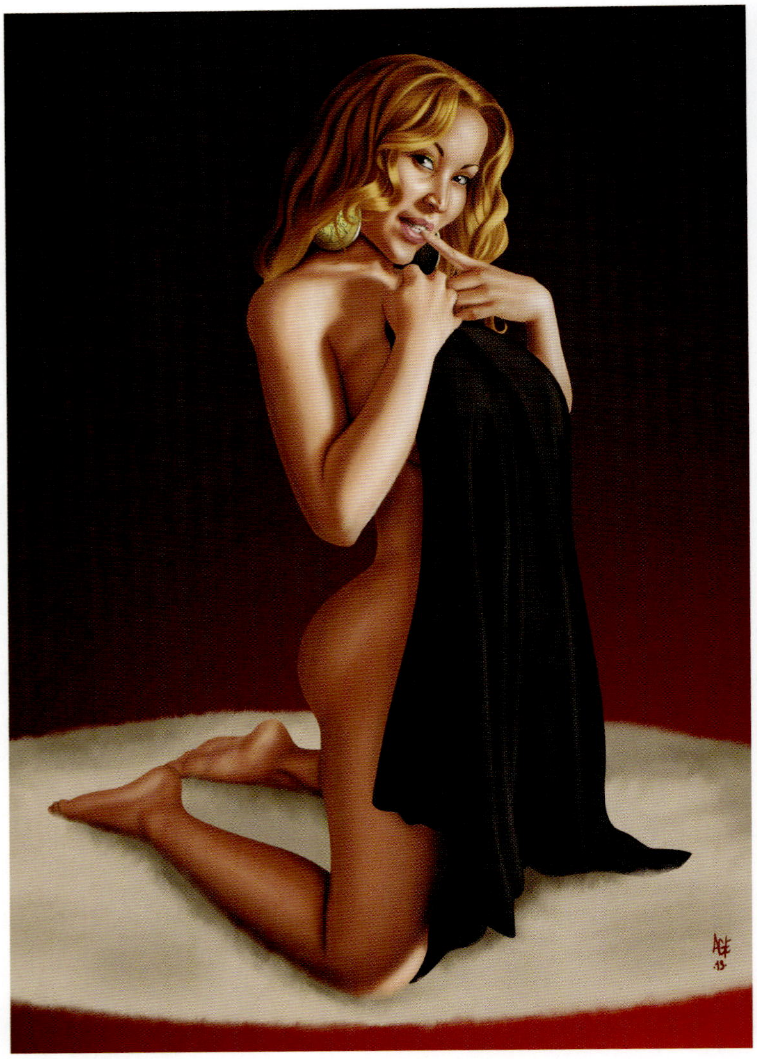

Precious Little Pin Up

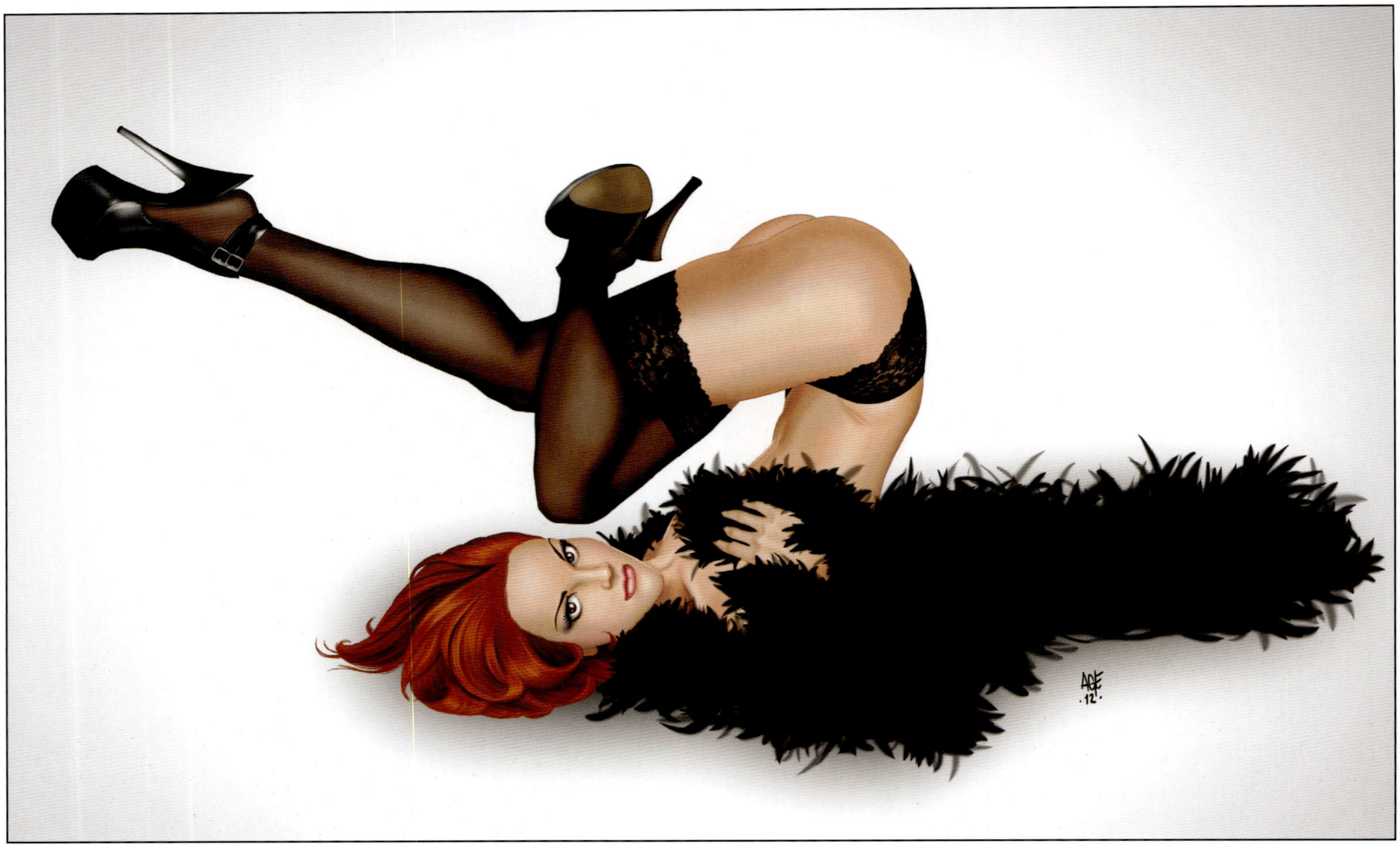

Feathers

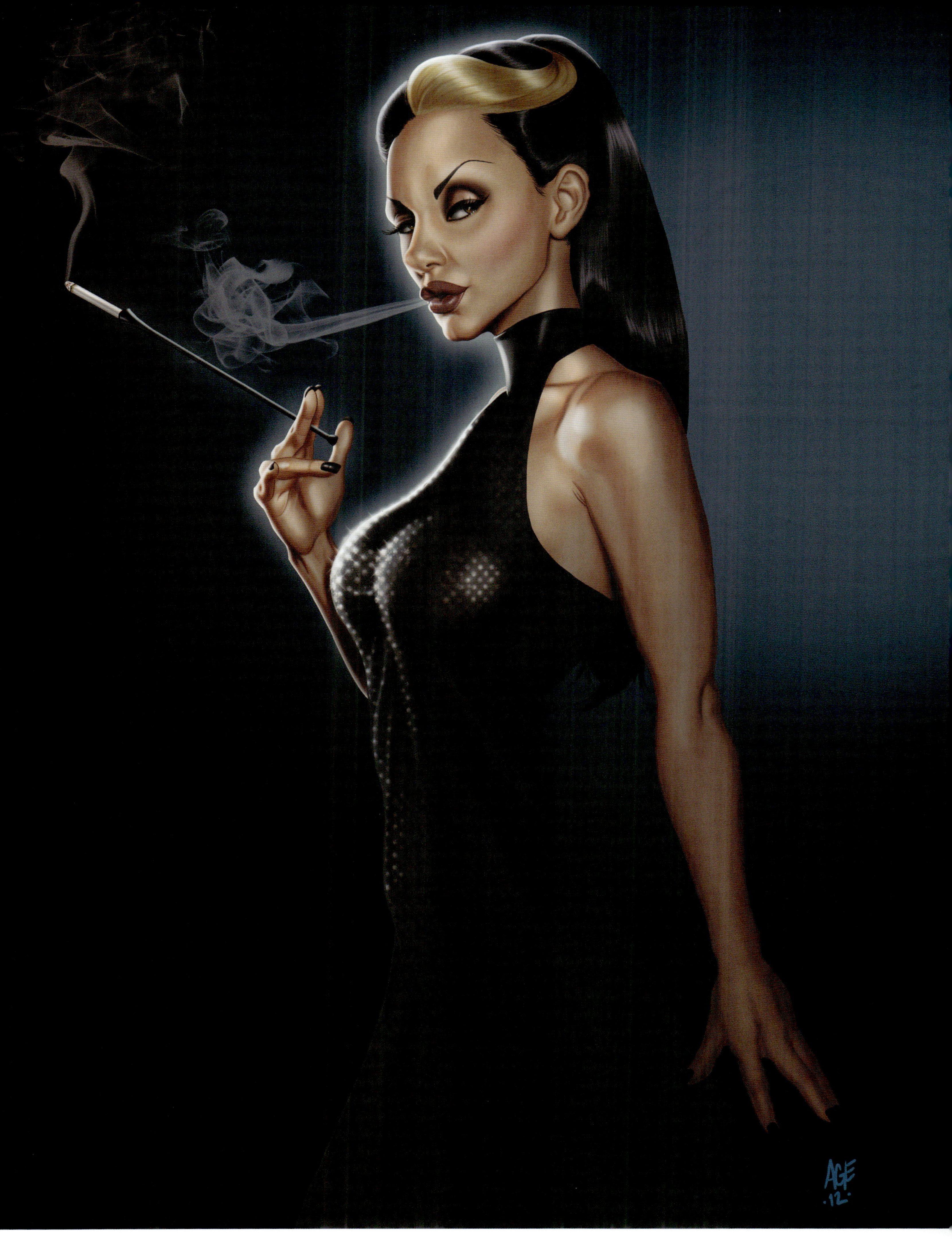

That Most Deadly Vice

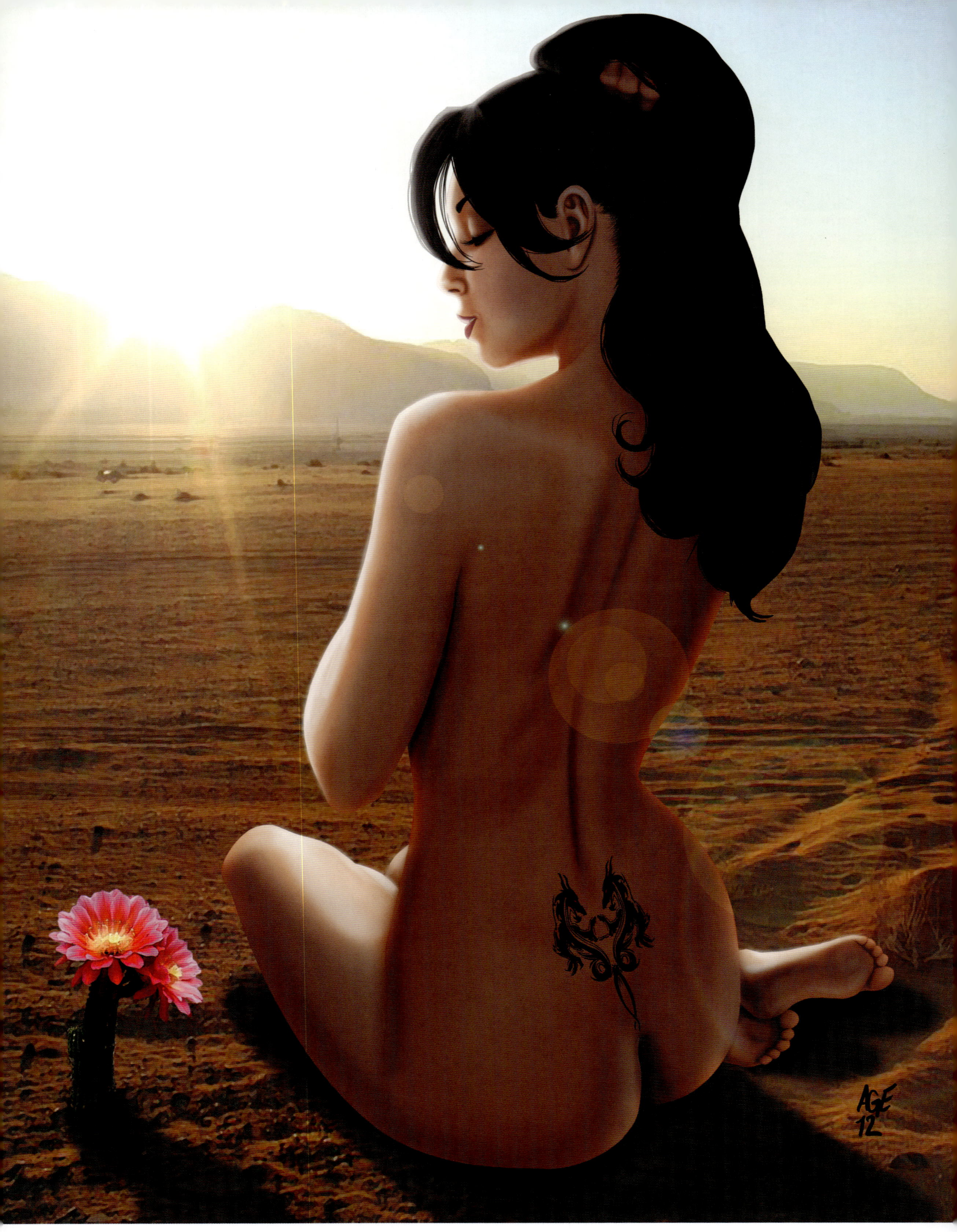

Desert Flower

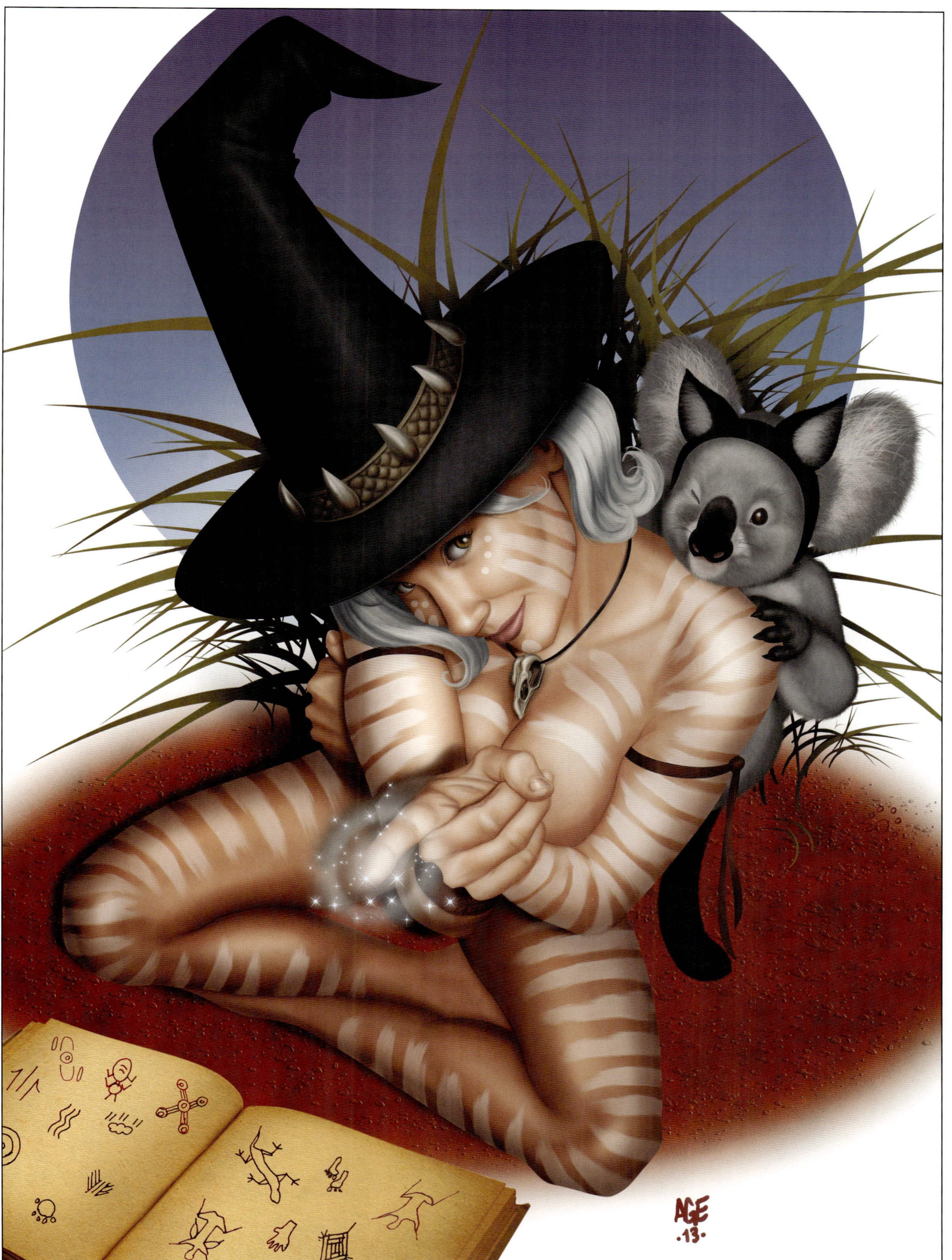

Outback Coven

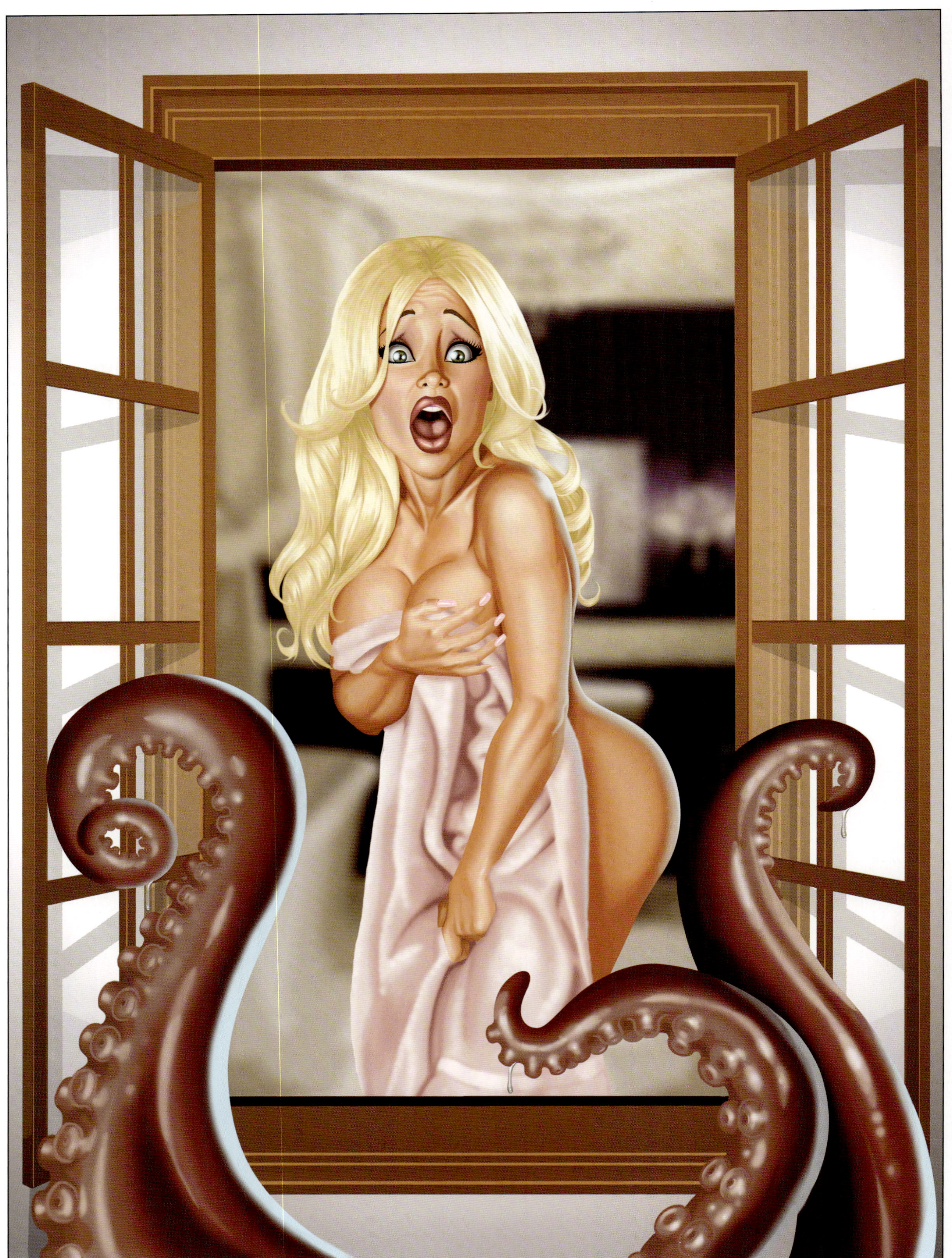

Monsters Never Knock

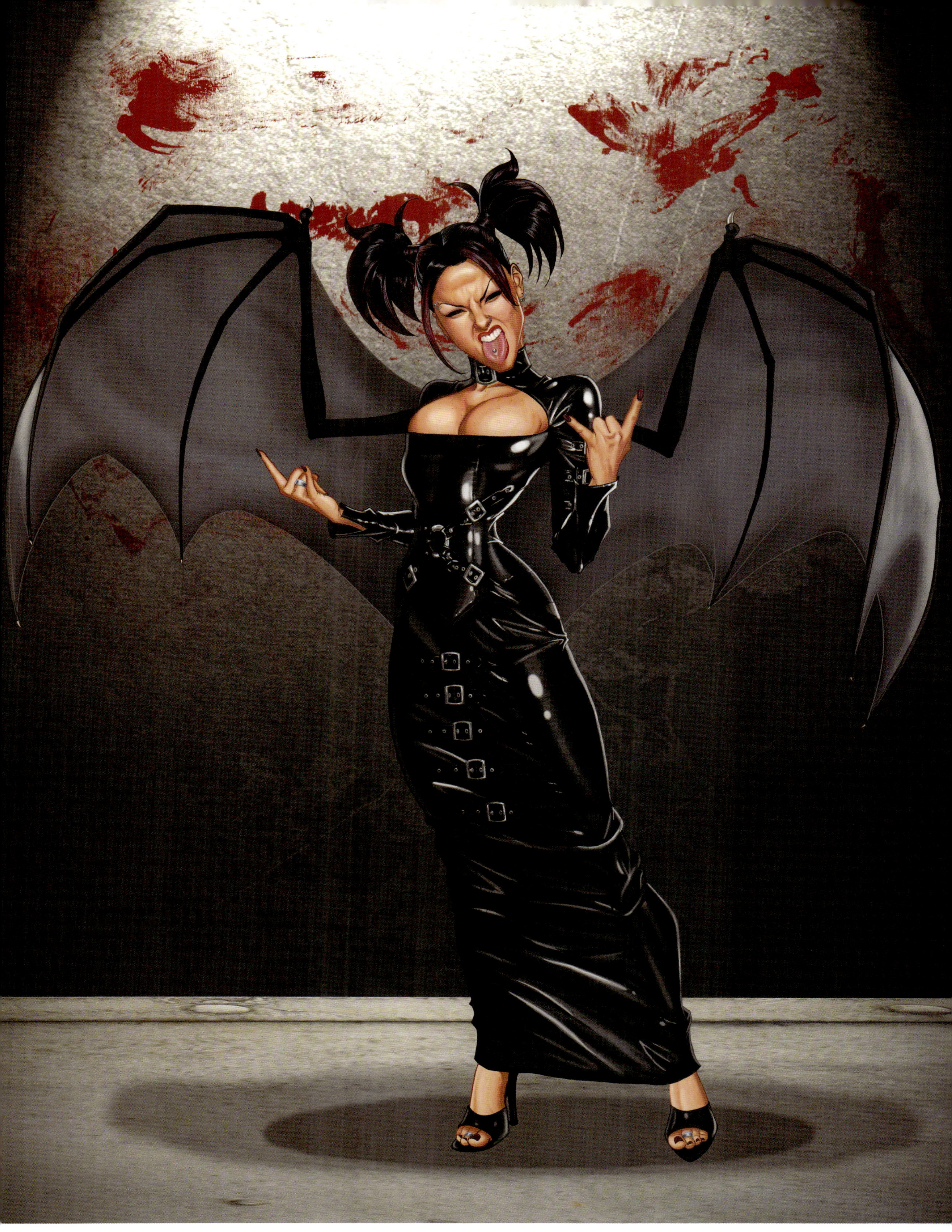

Queen of the Damned

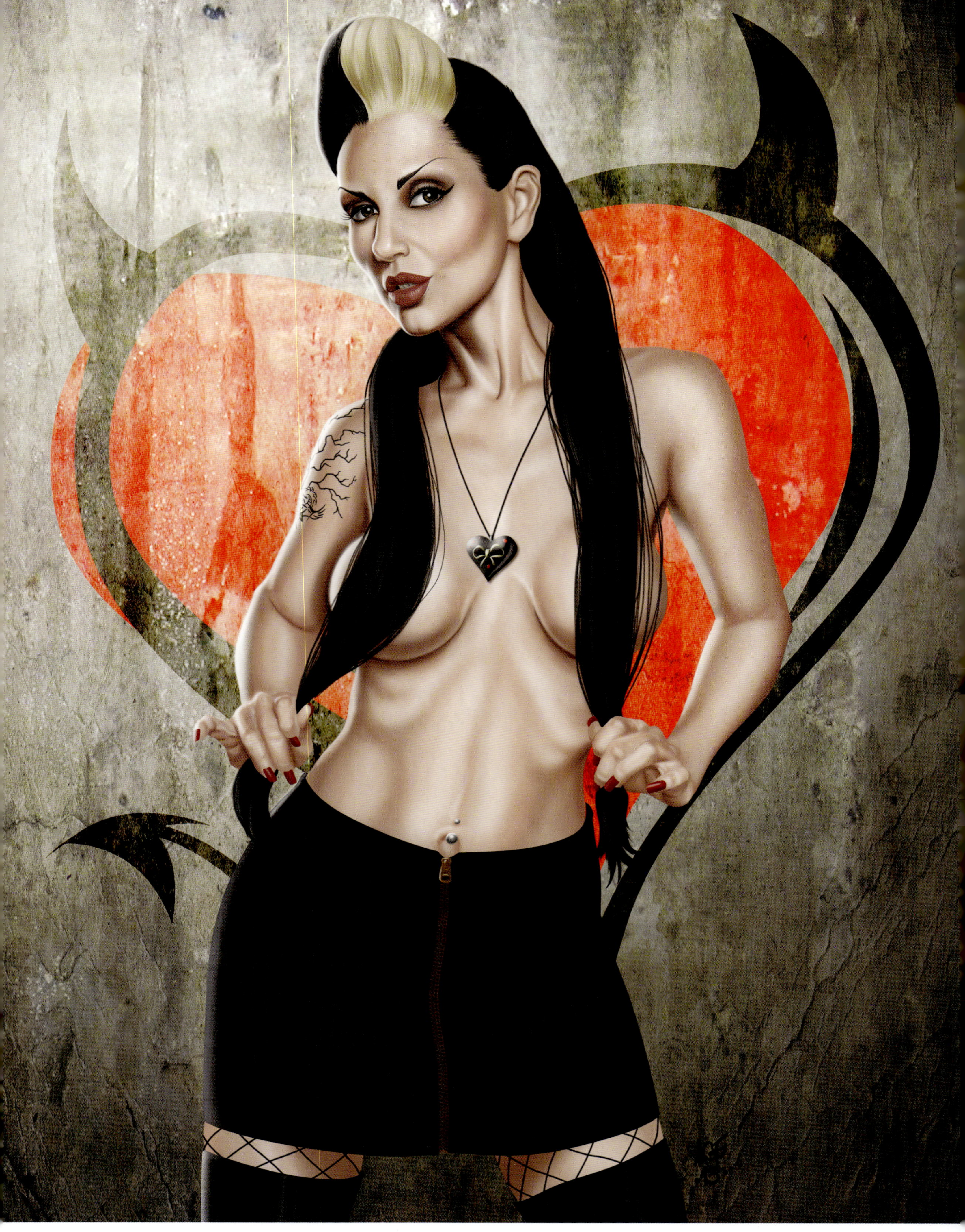

Graffiti

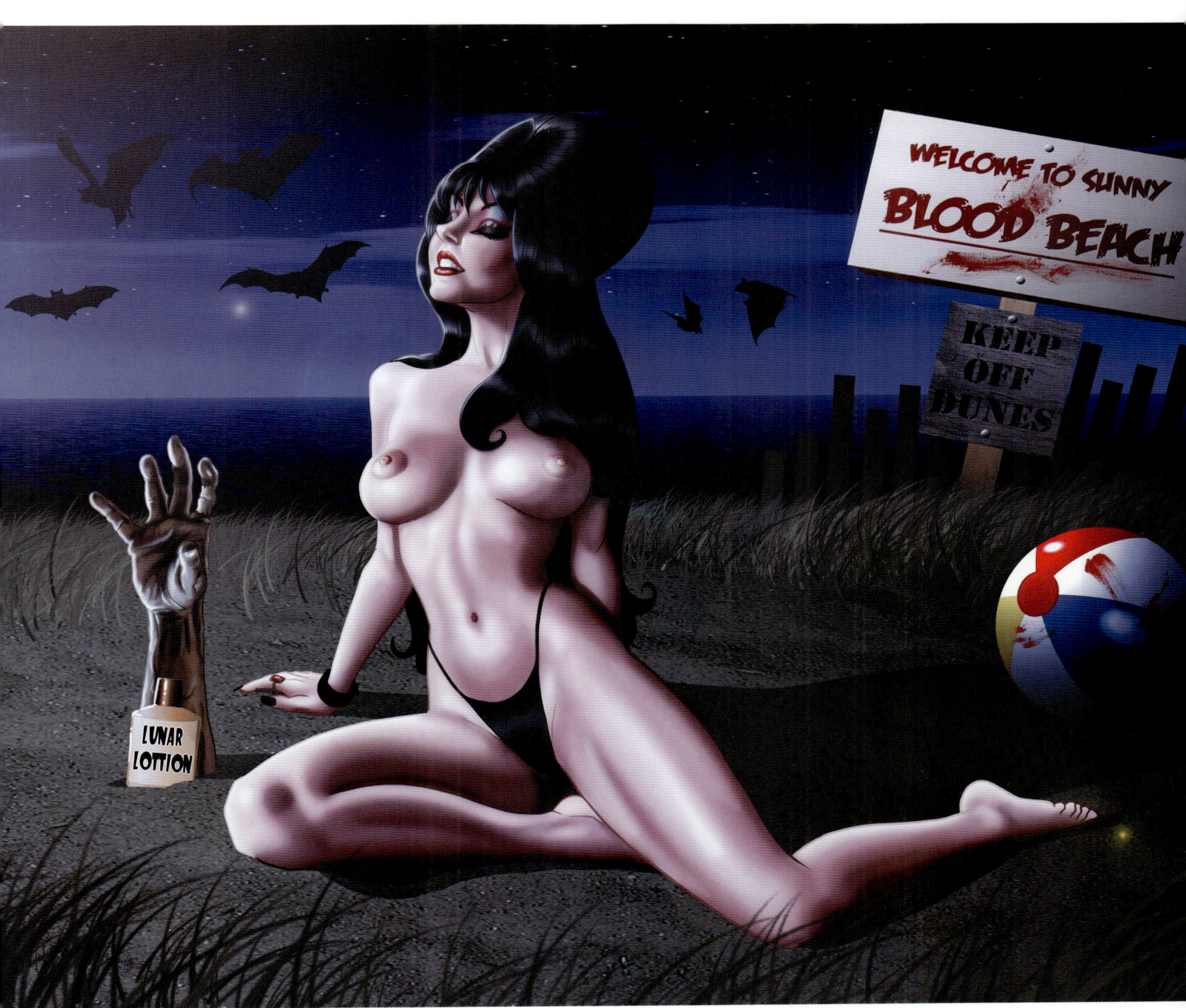

Moon Tan

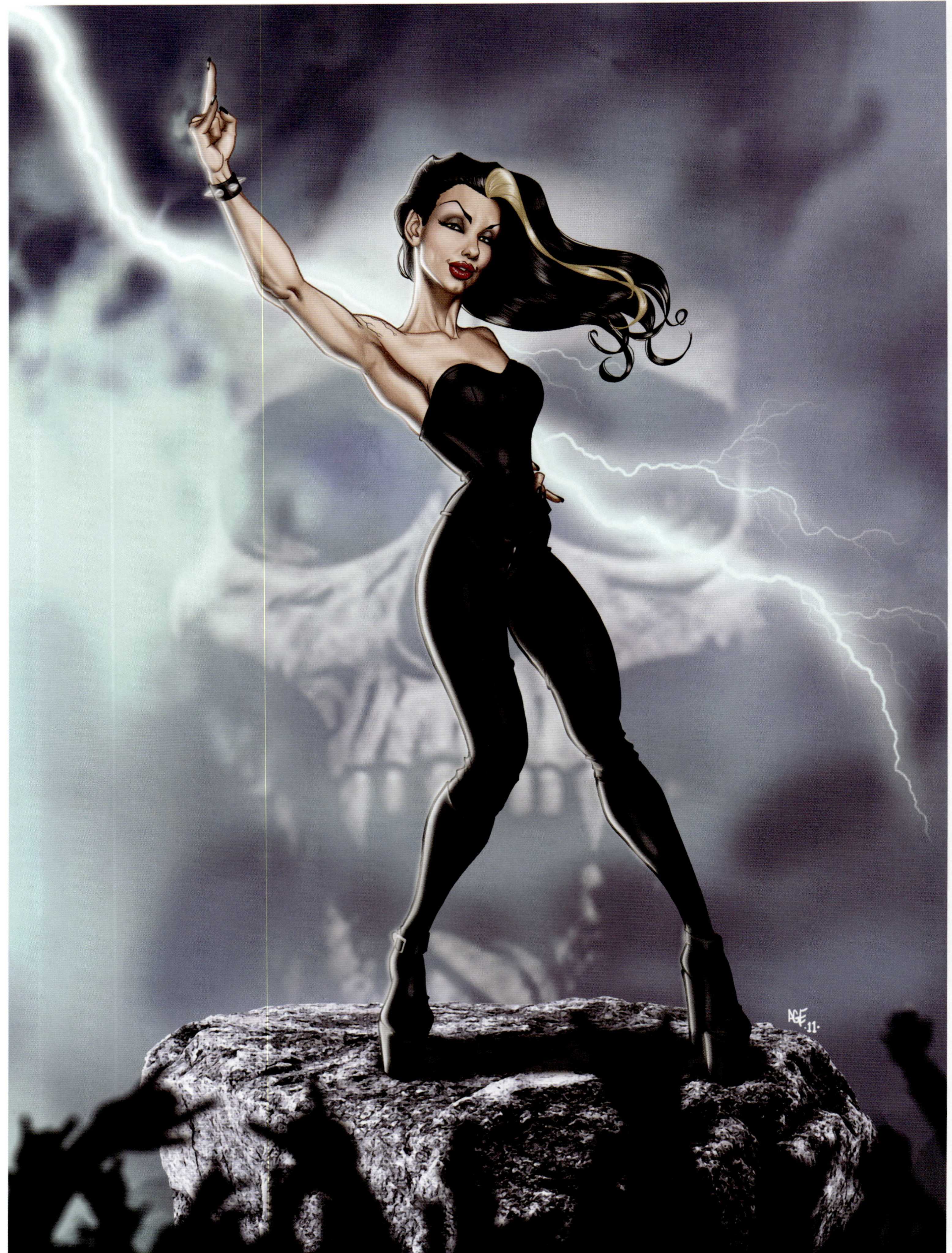

Rock It To Hell

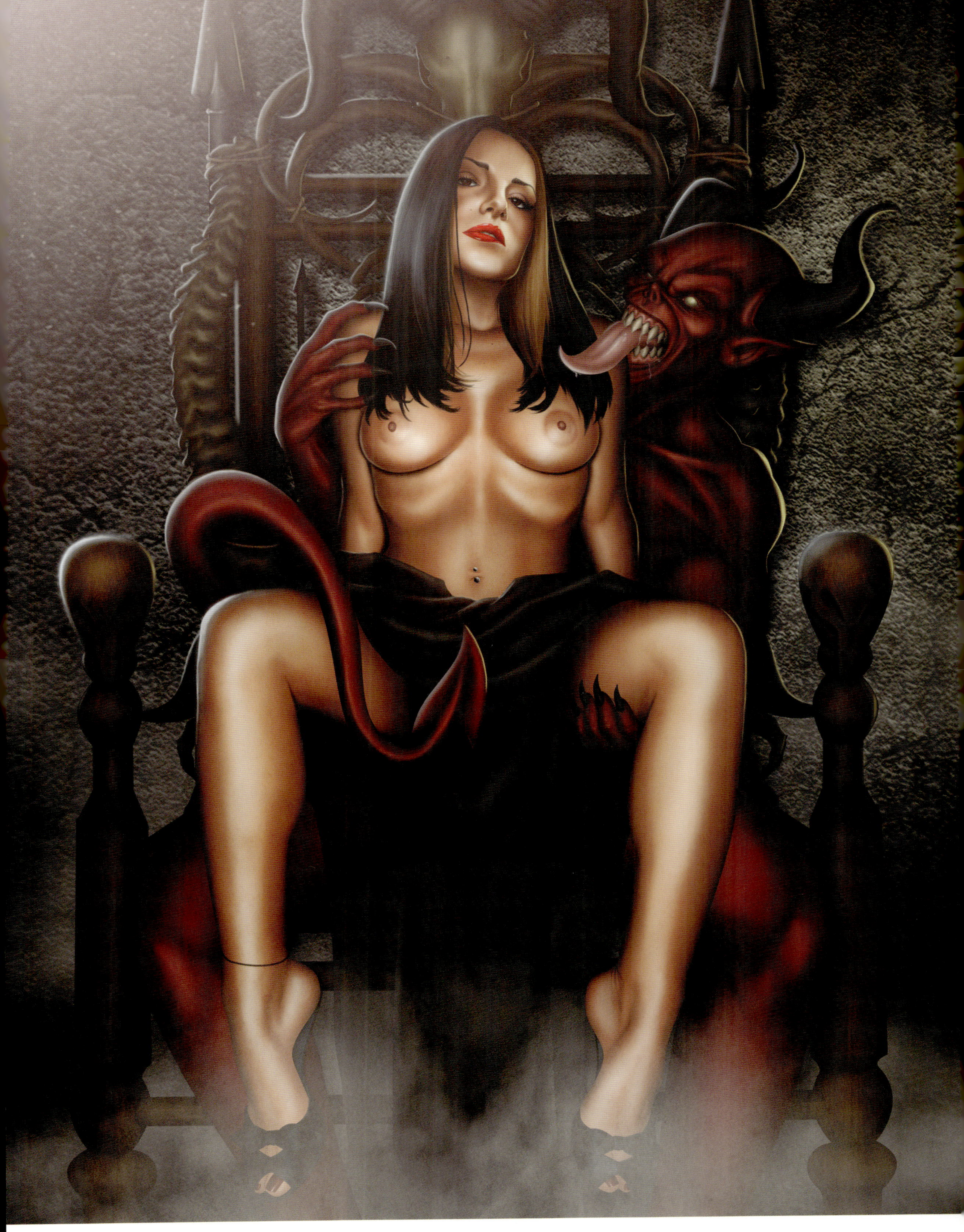

666th Lover

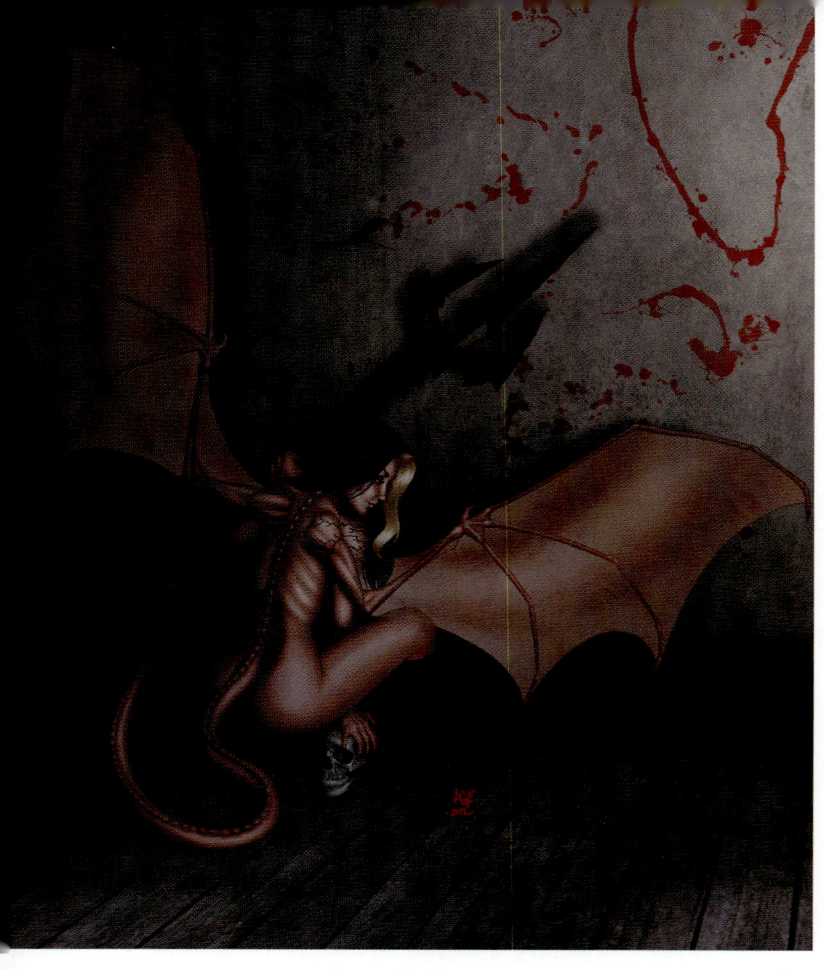

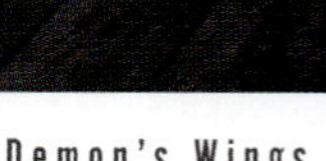

Demon's Wings

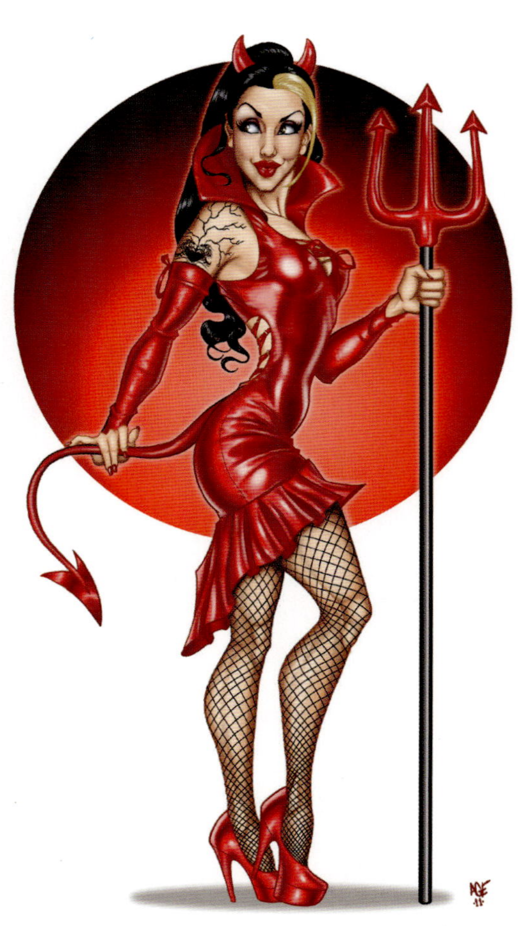

Devil Girl

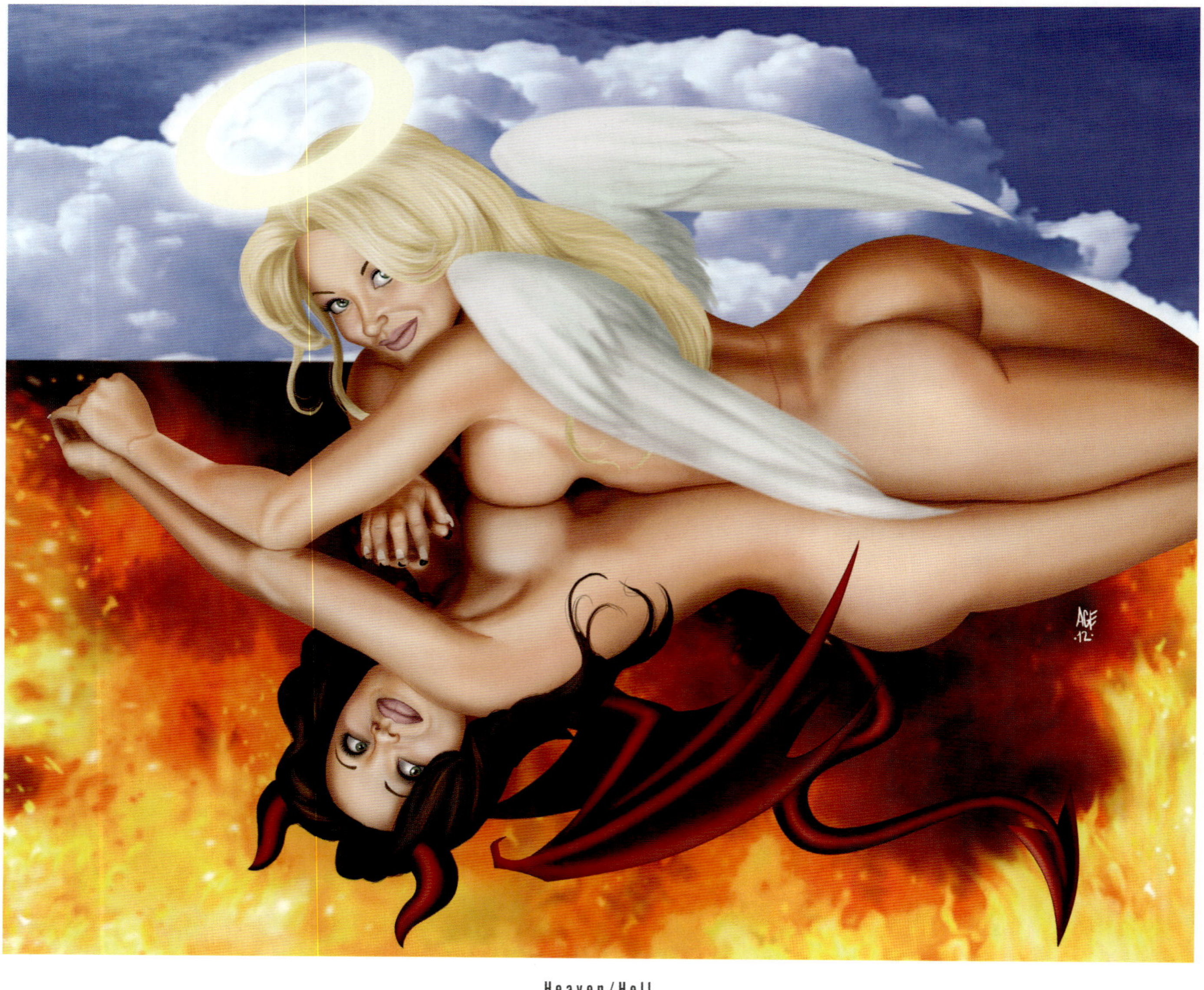

Heaven/Hell

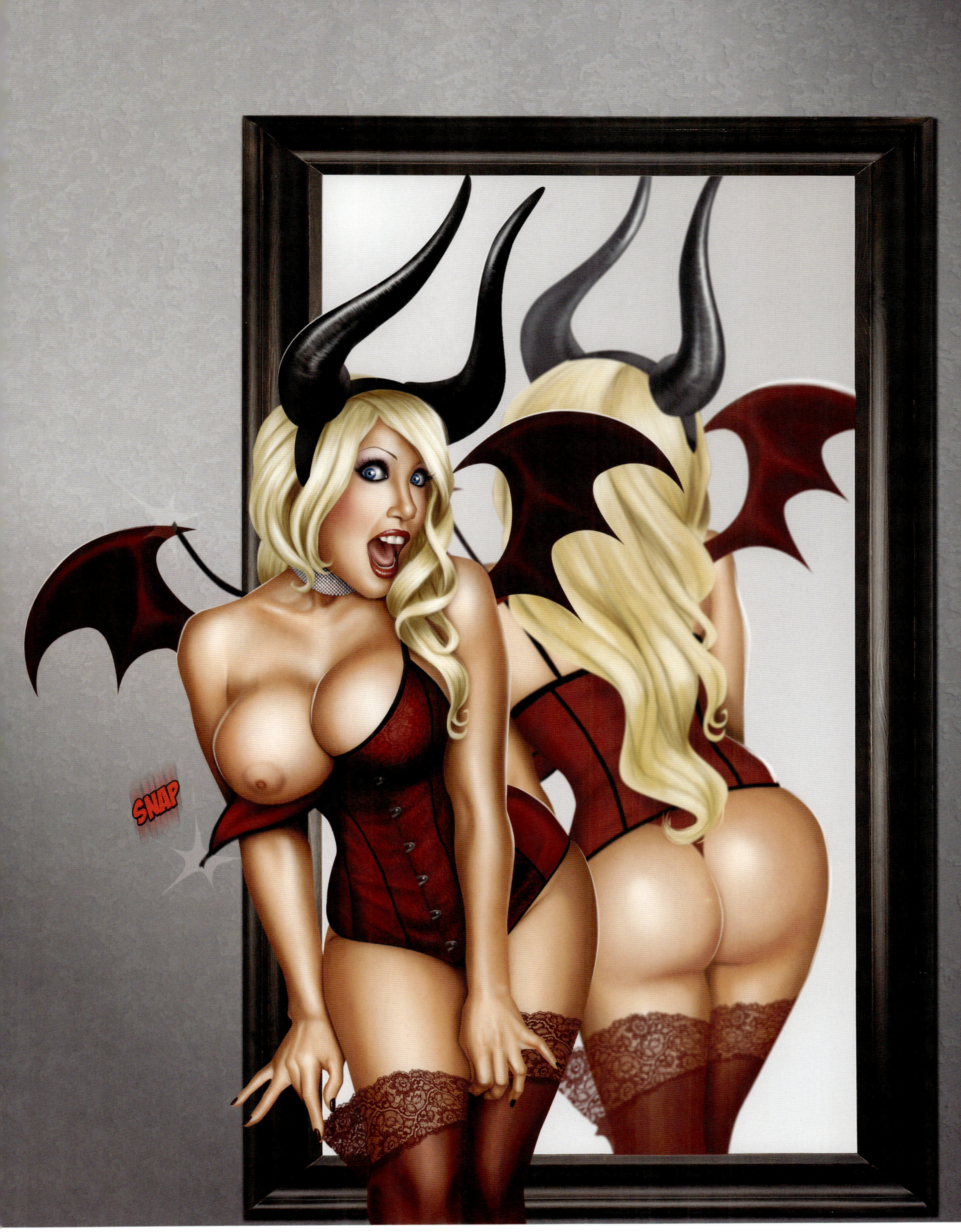

Oopsie!

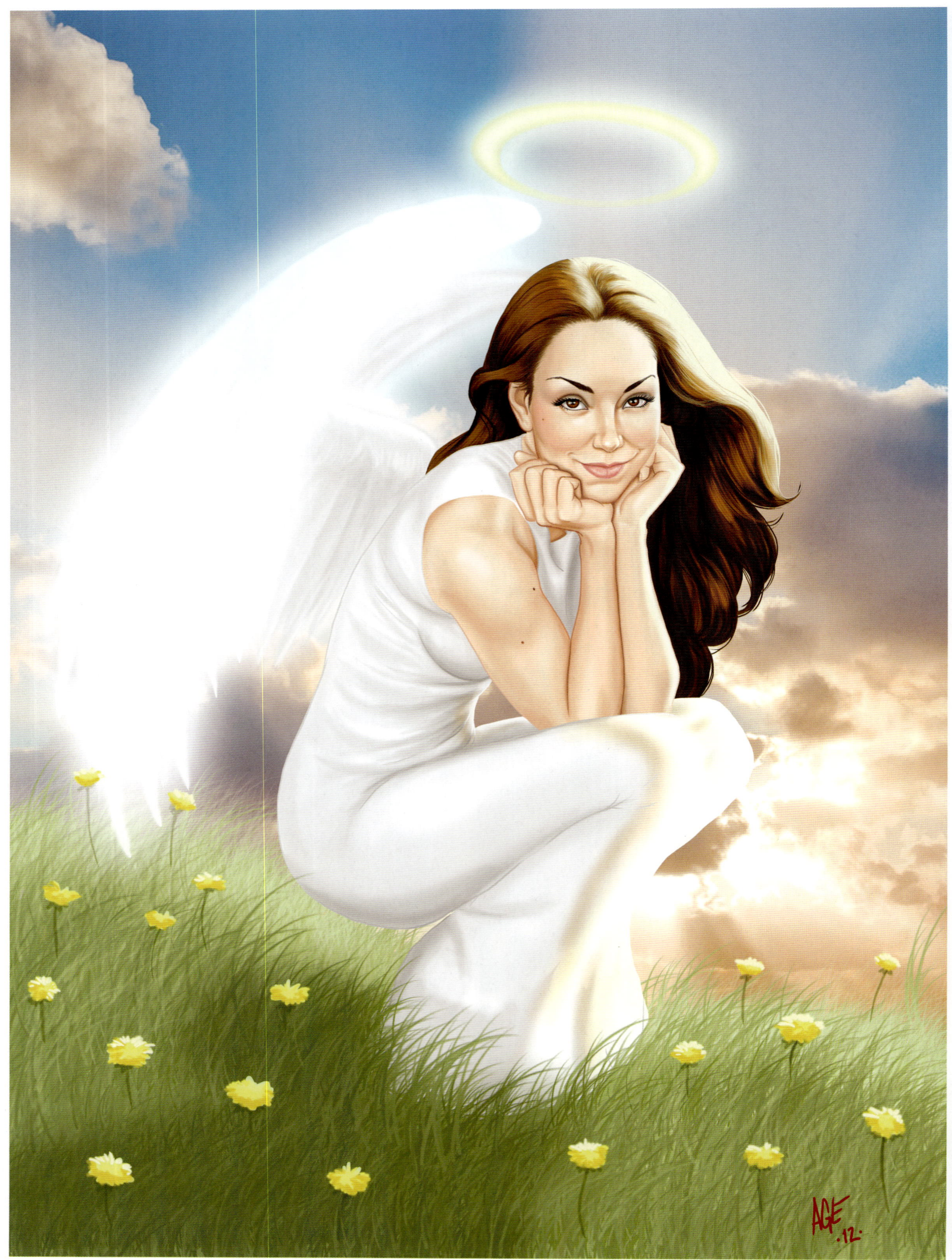

Angel Eyes

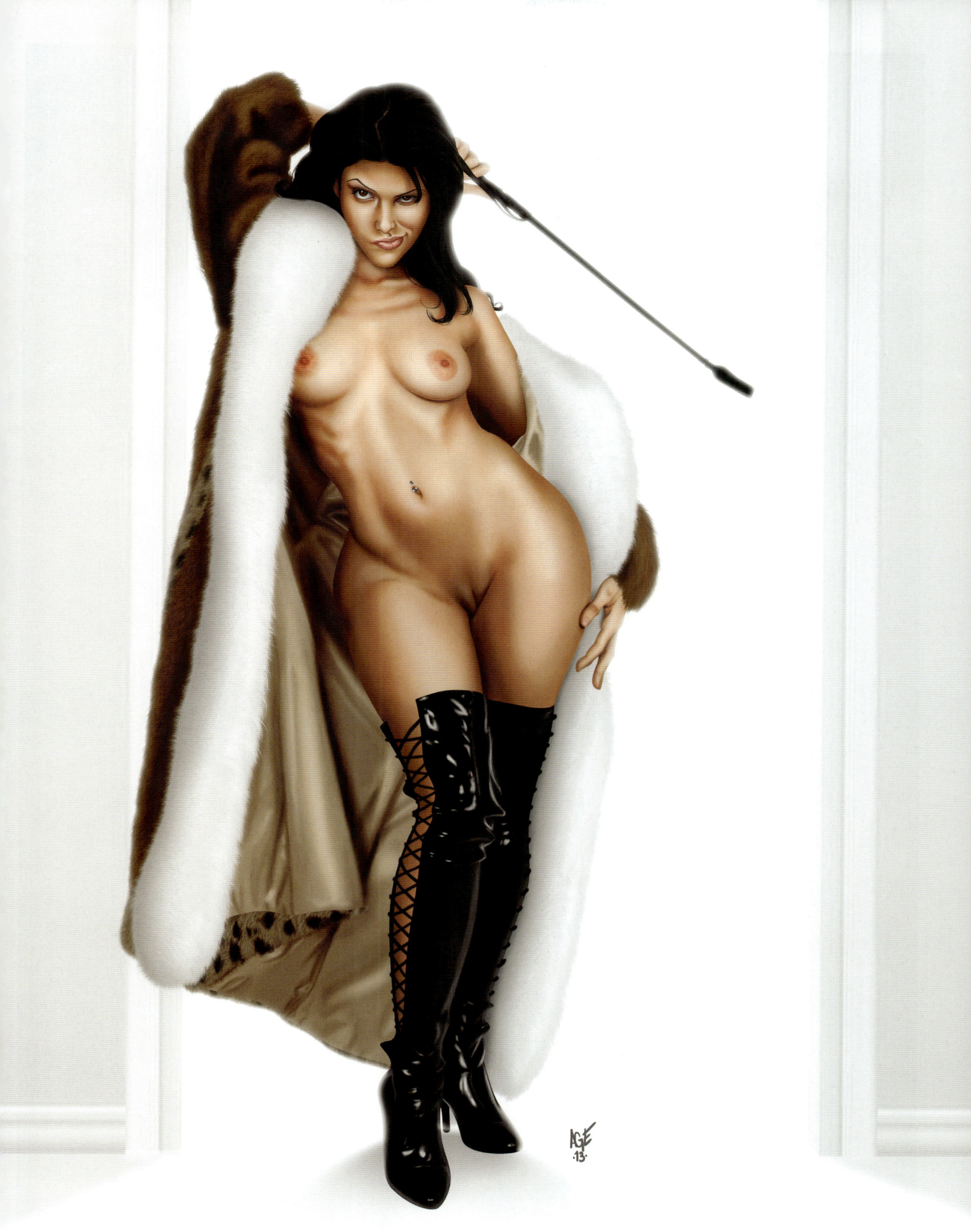

Dressed for Excess

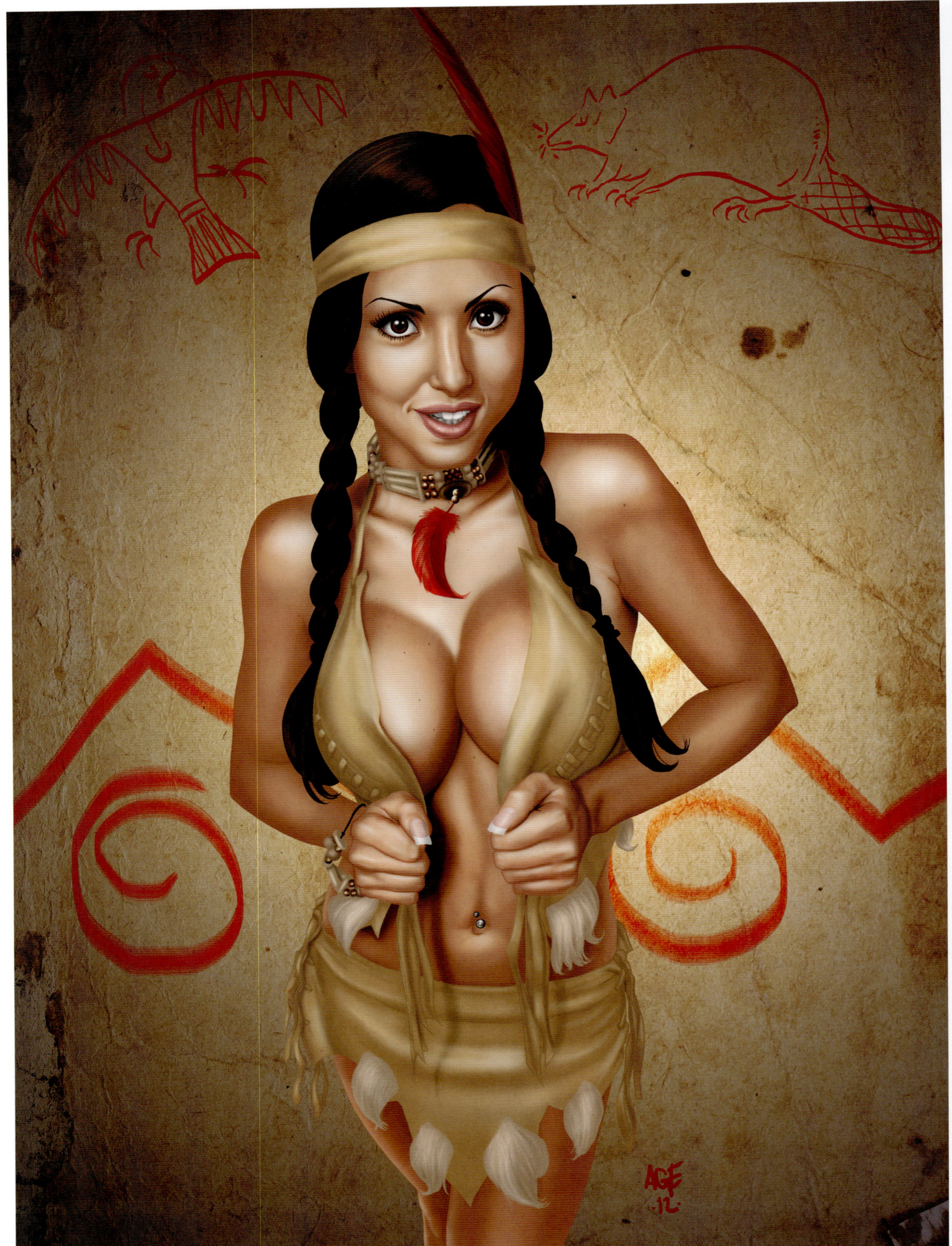

Native

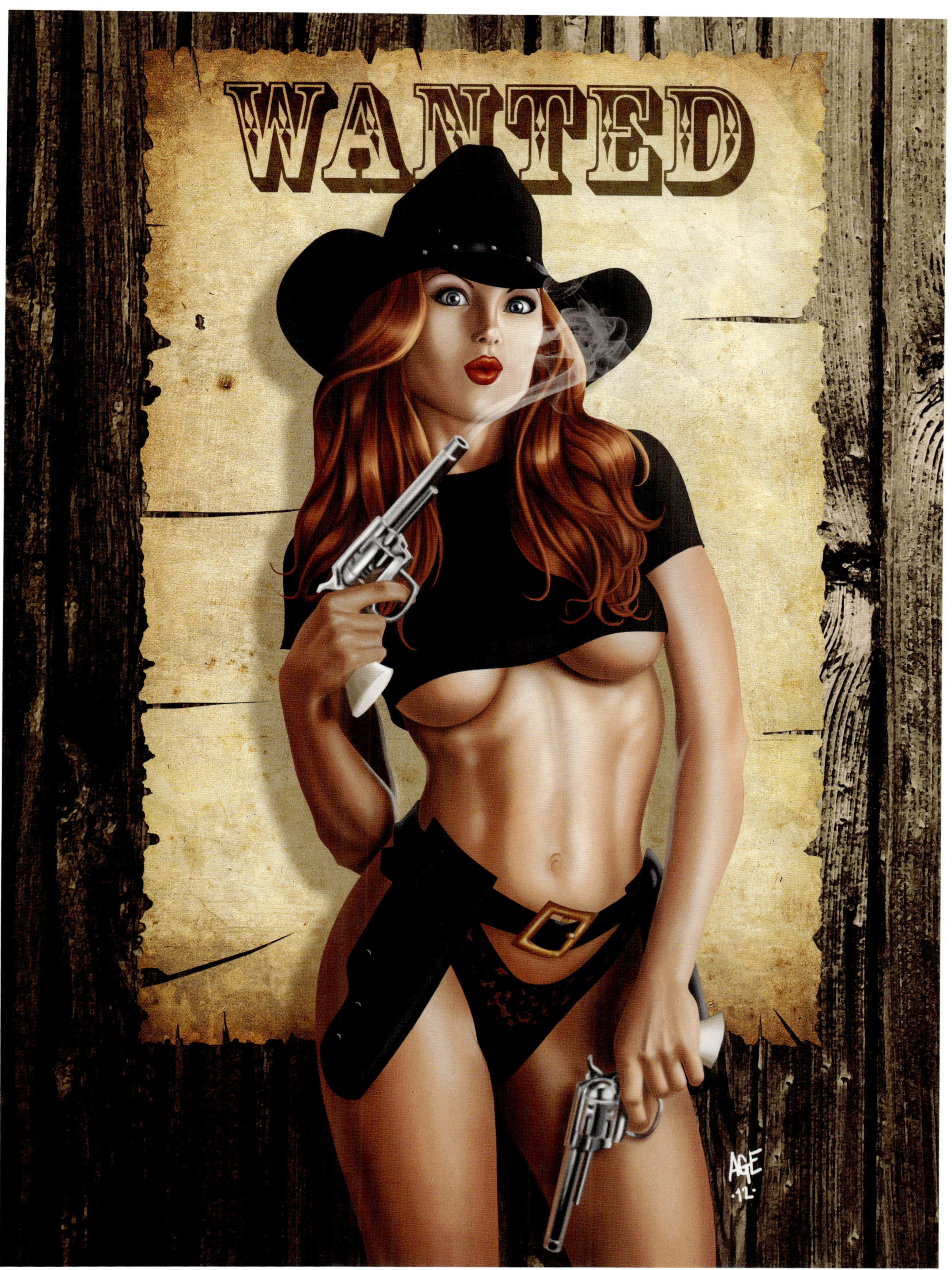

Gunsmokin' Hot

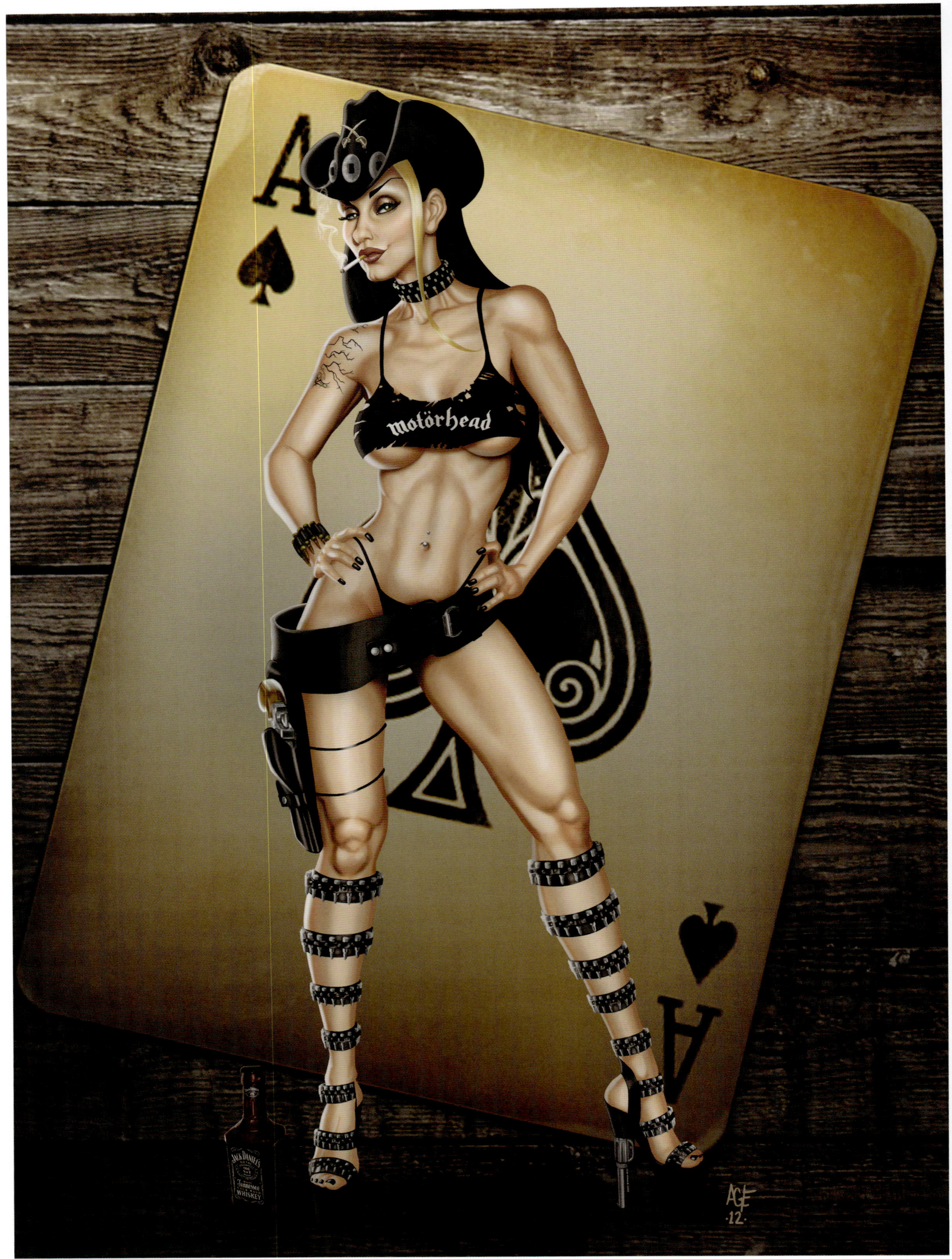

Ace of Spades

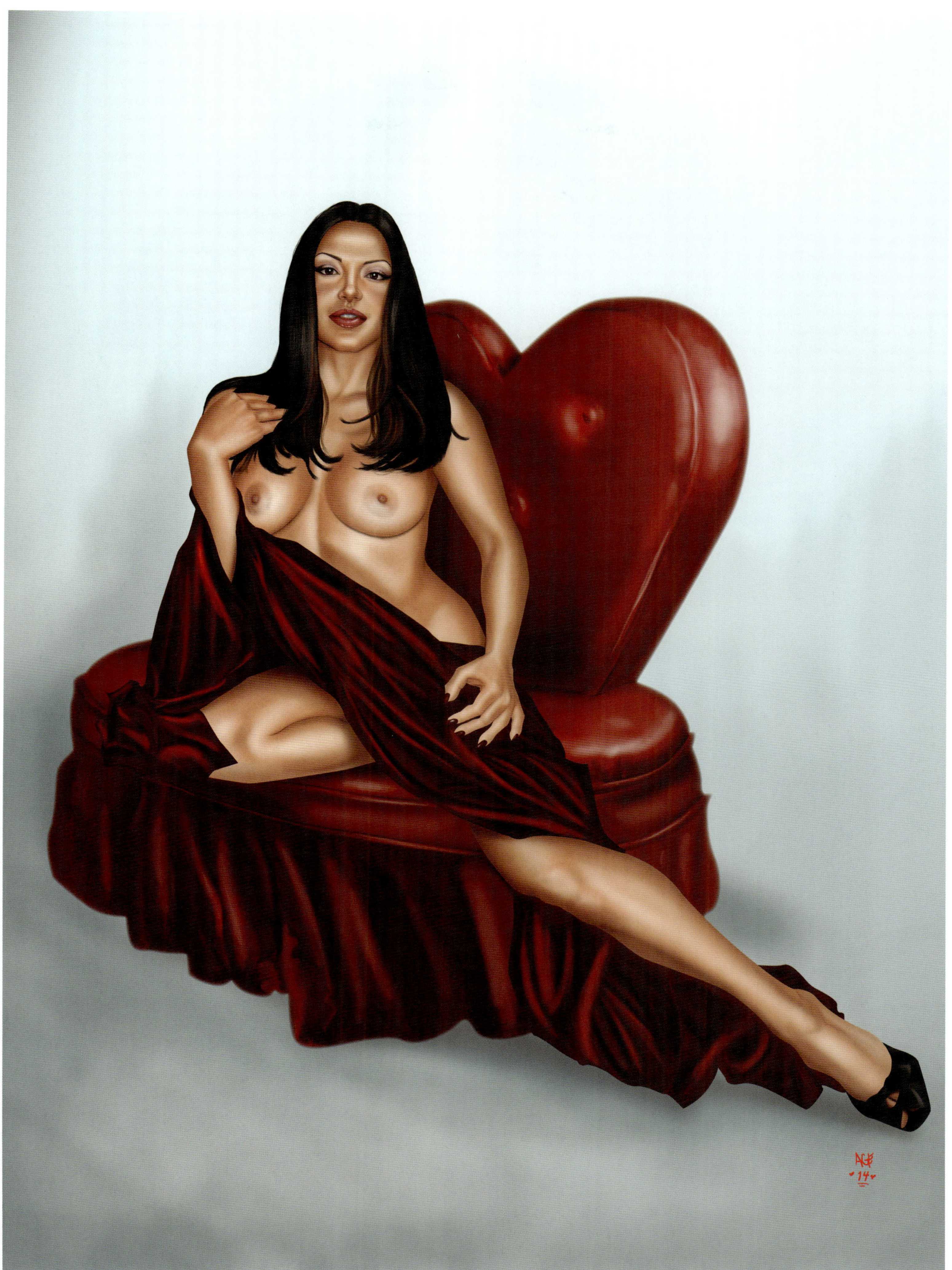

Elvgren Tribute

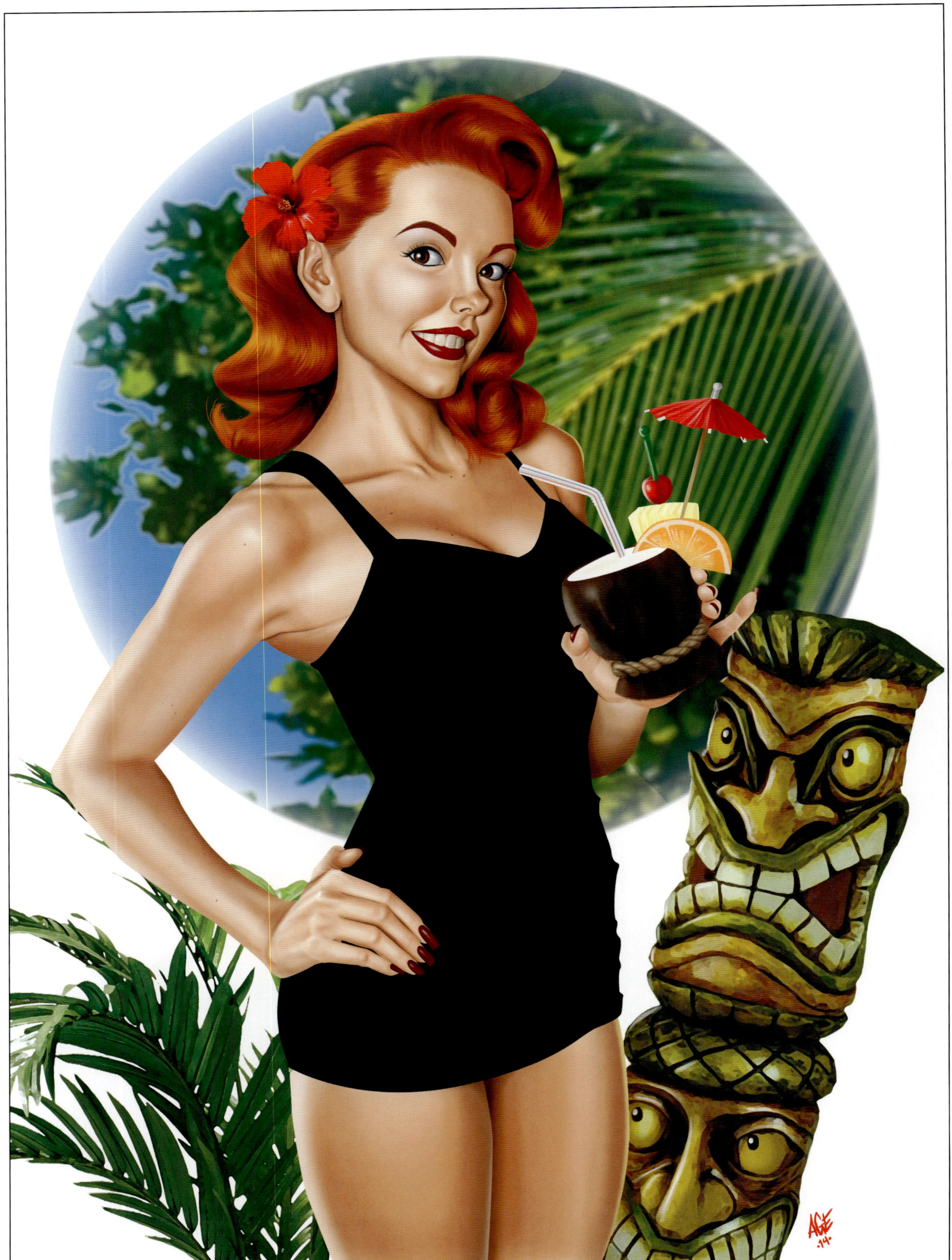

Vintage Tiki

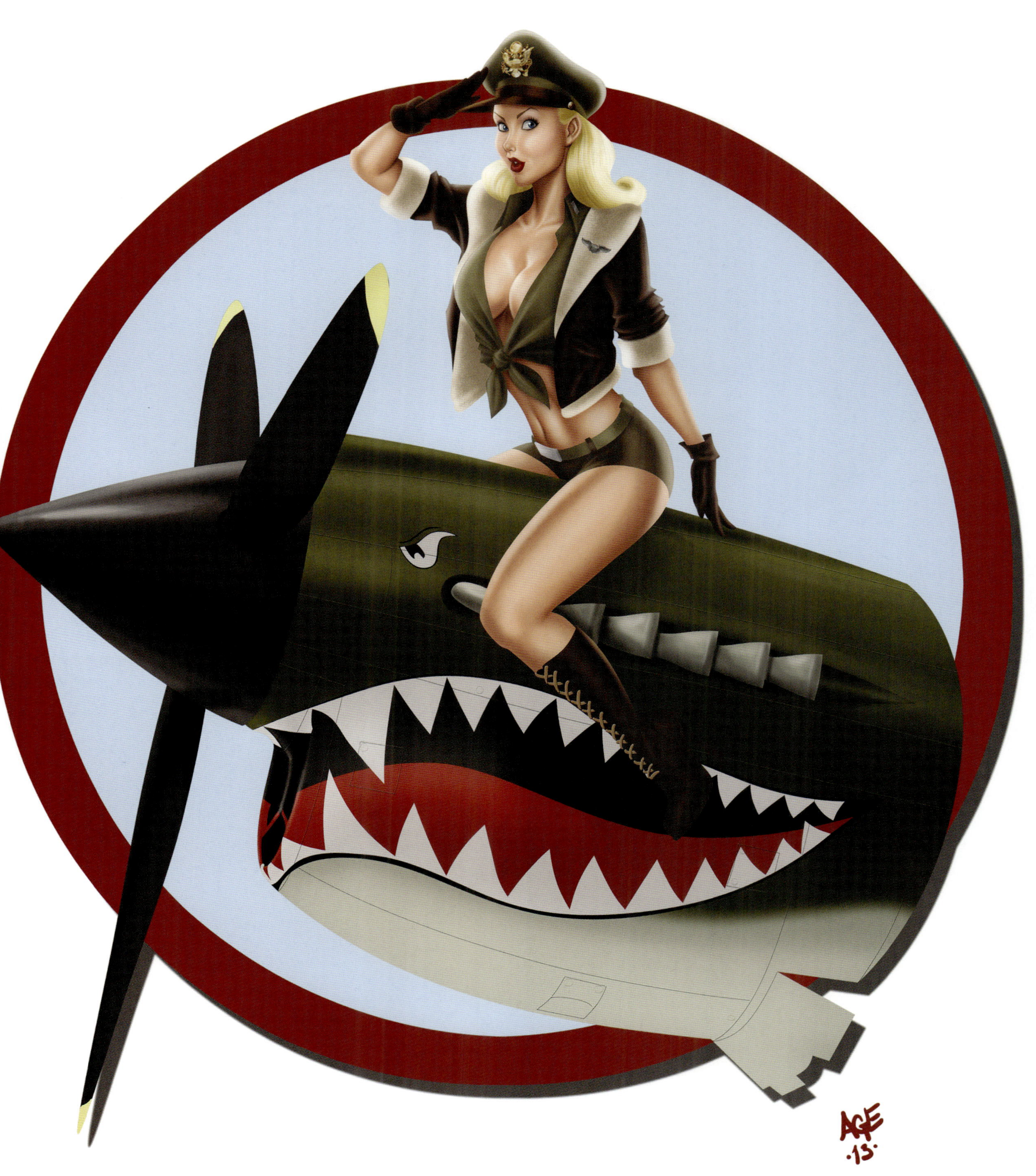

Bombshell Bomber

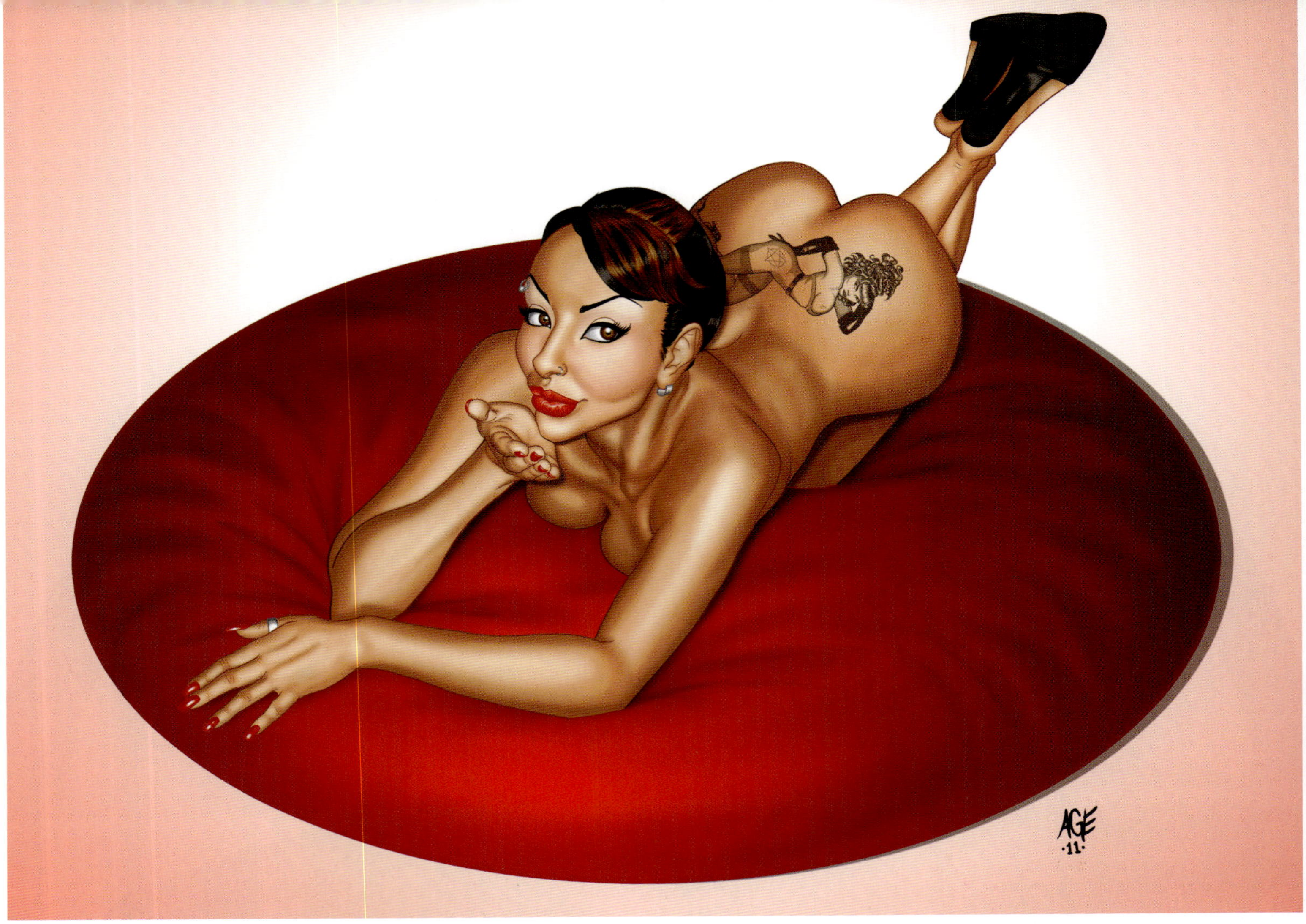

Affectionately Yours

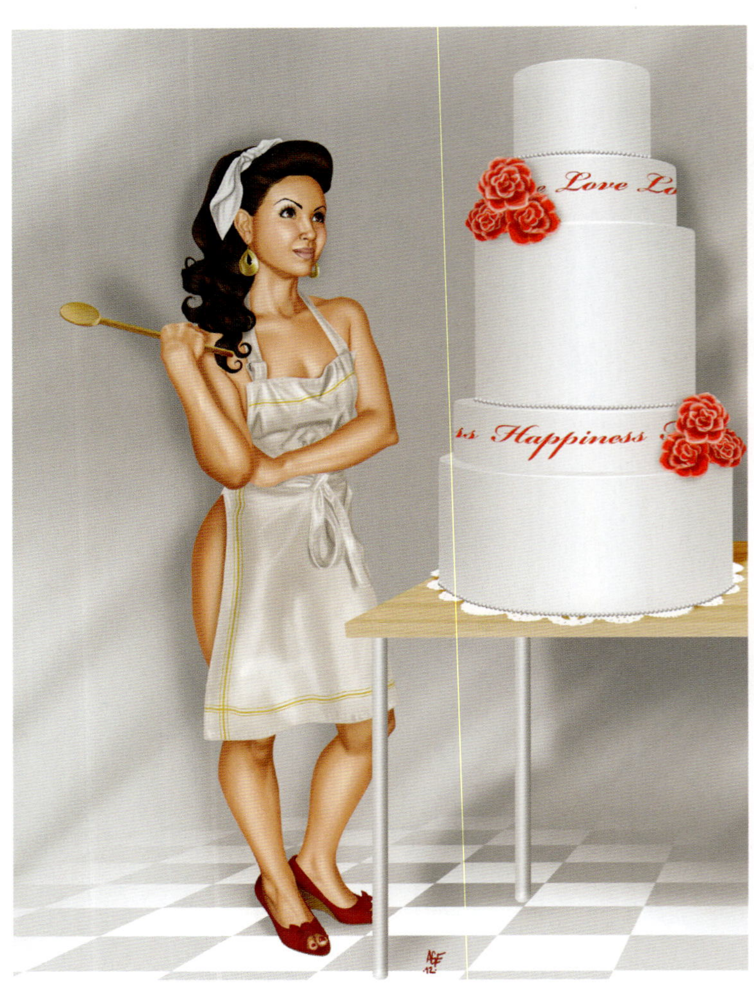

Hard to Top

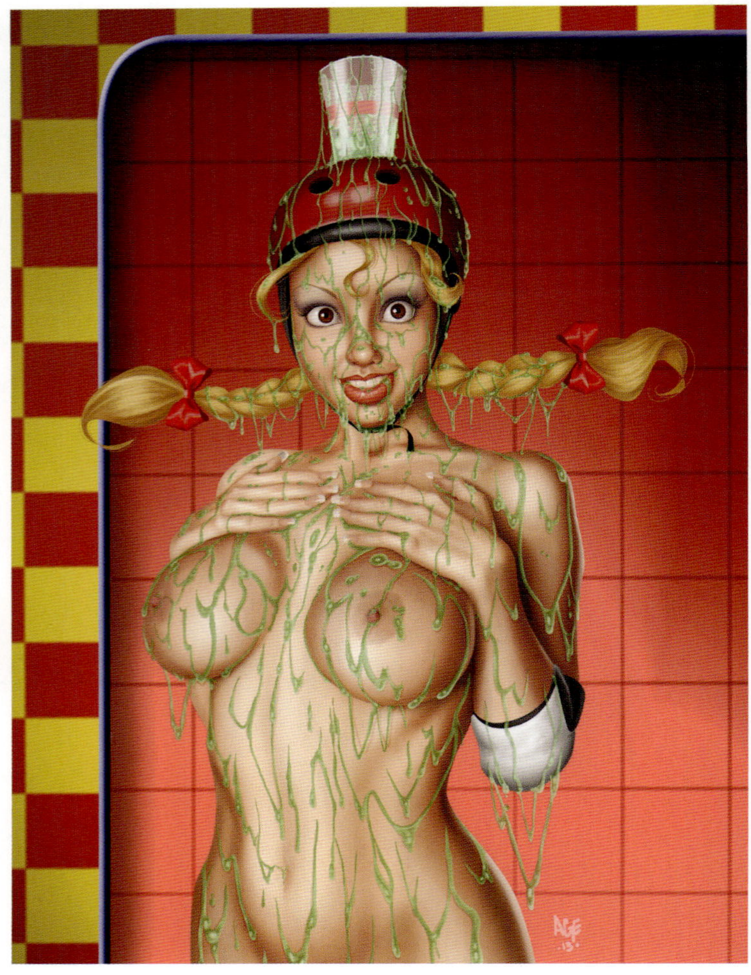

Double Dare

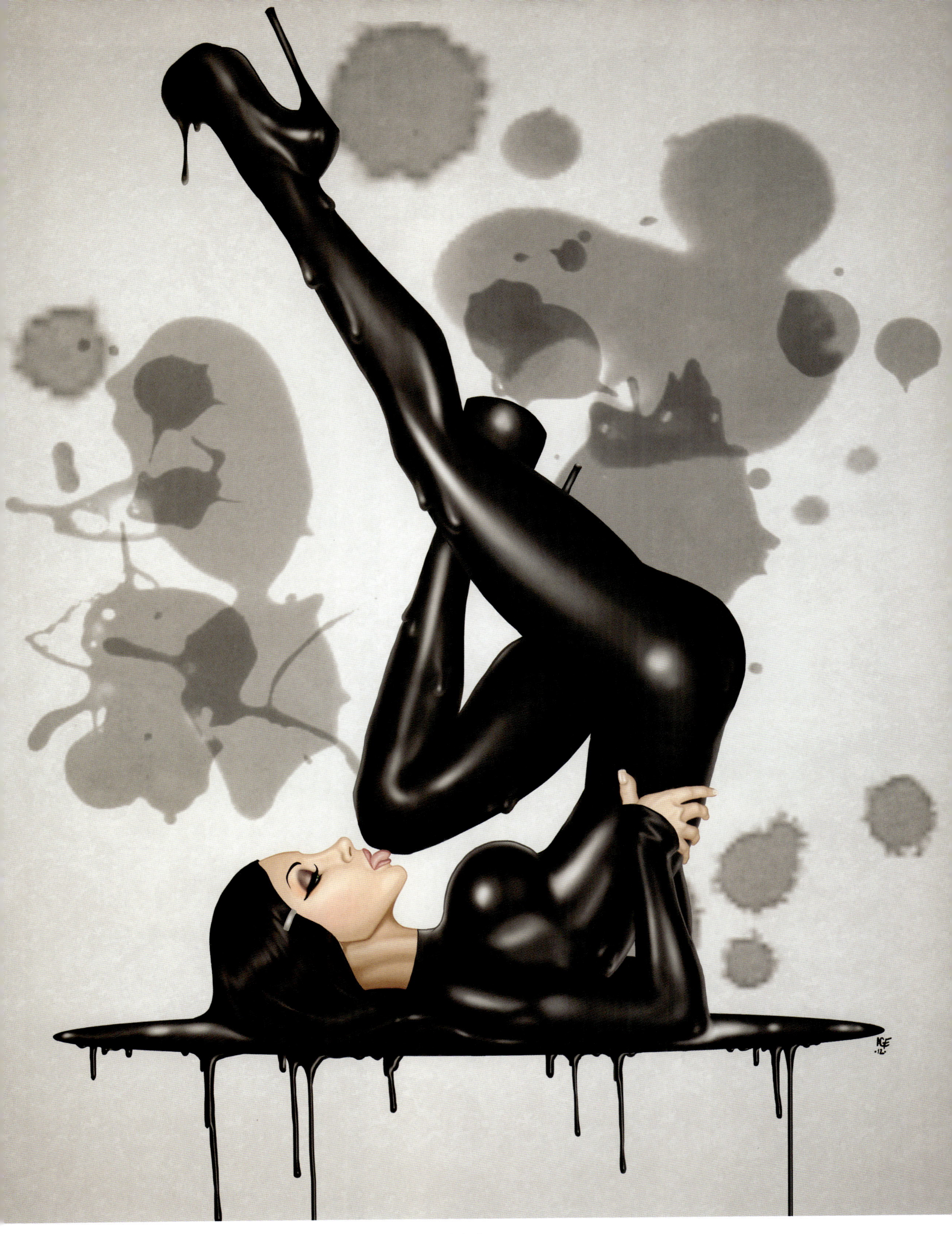

Inked

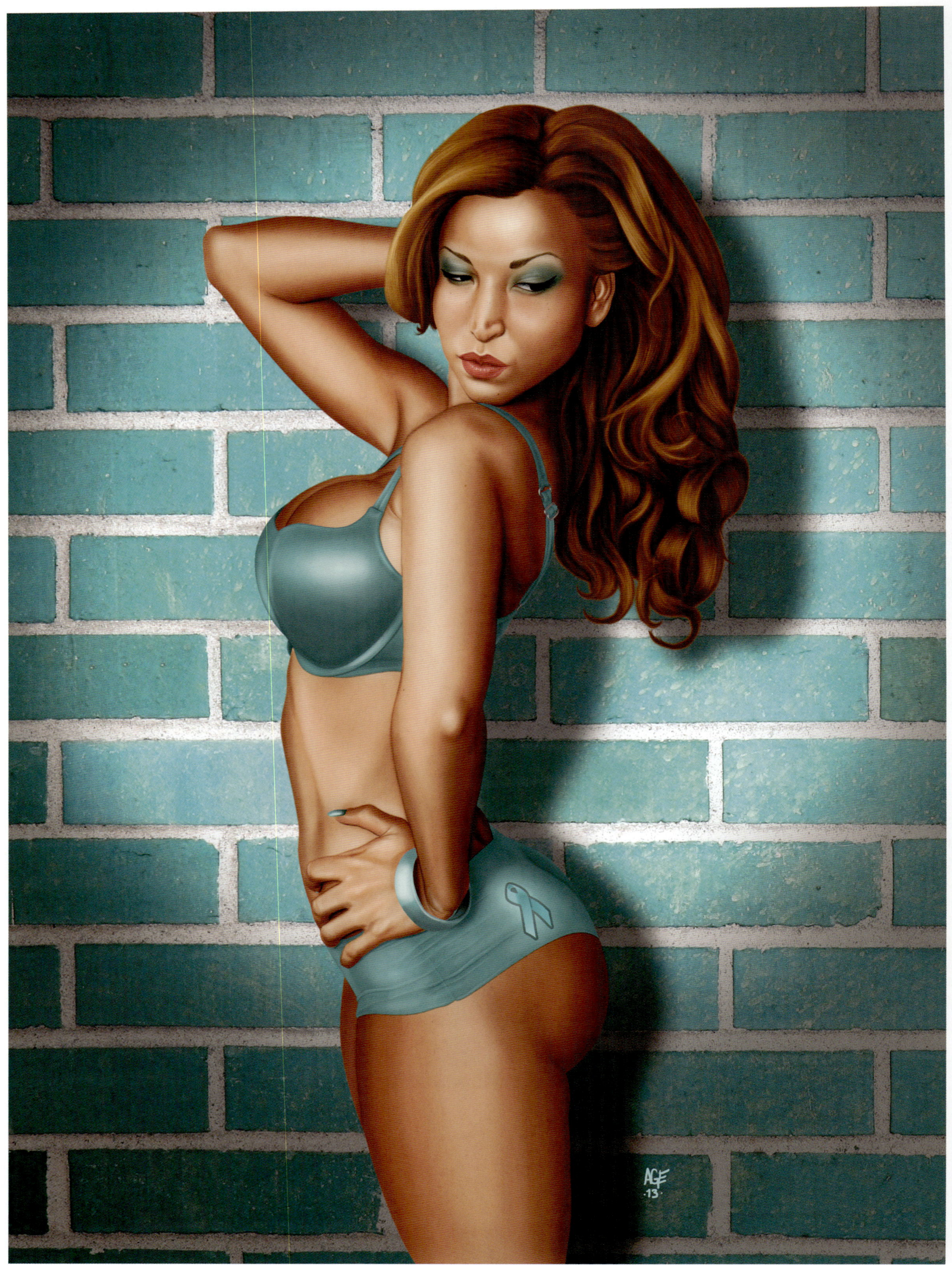

Teal

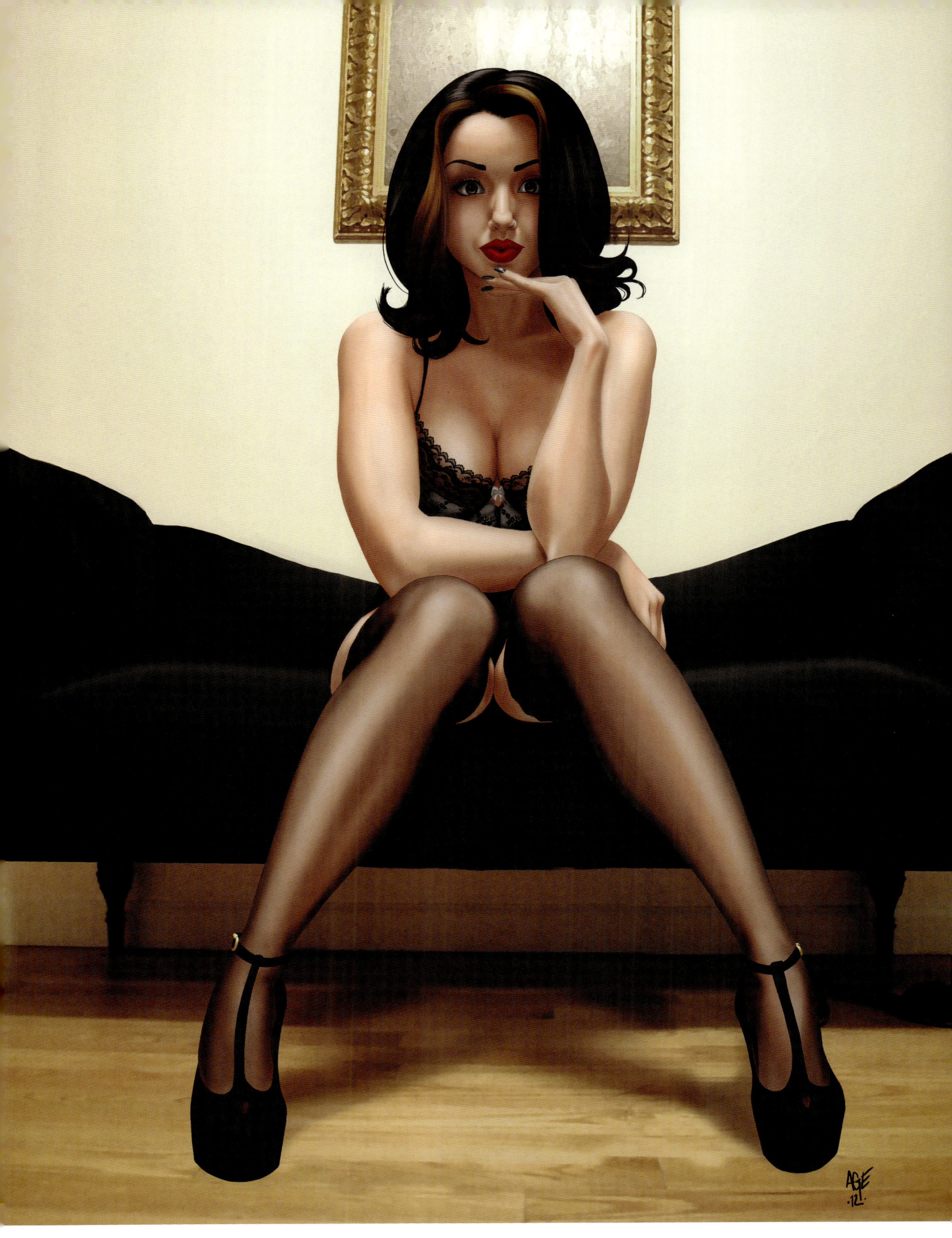
AGE
·12·

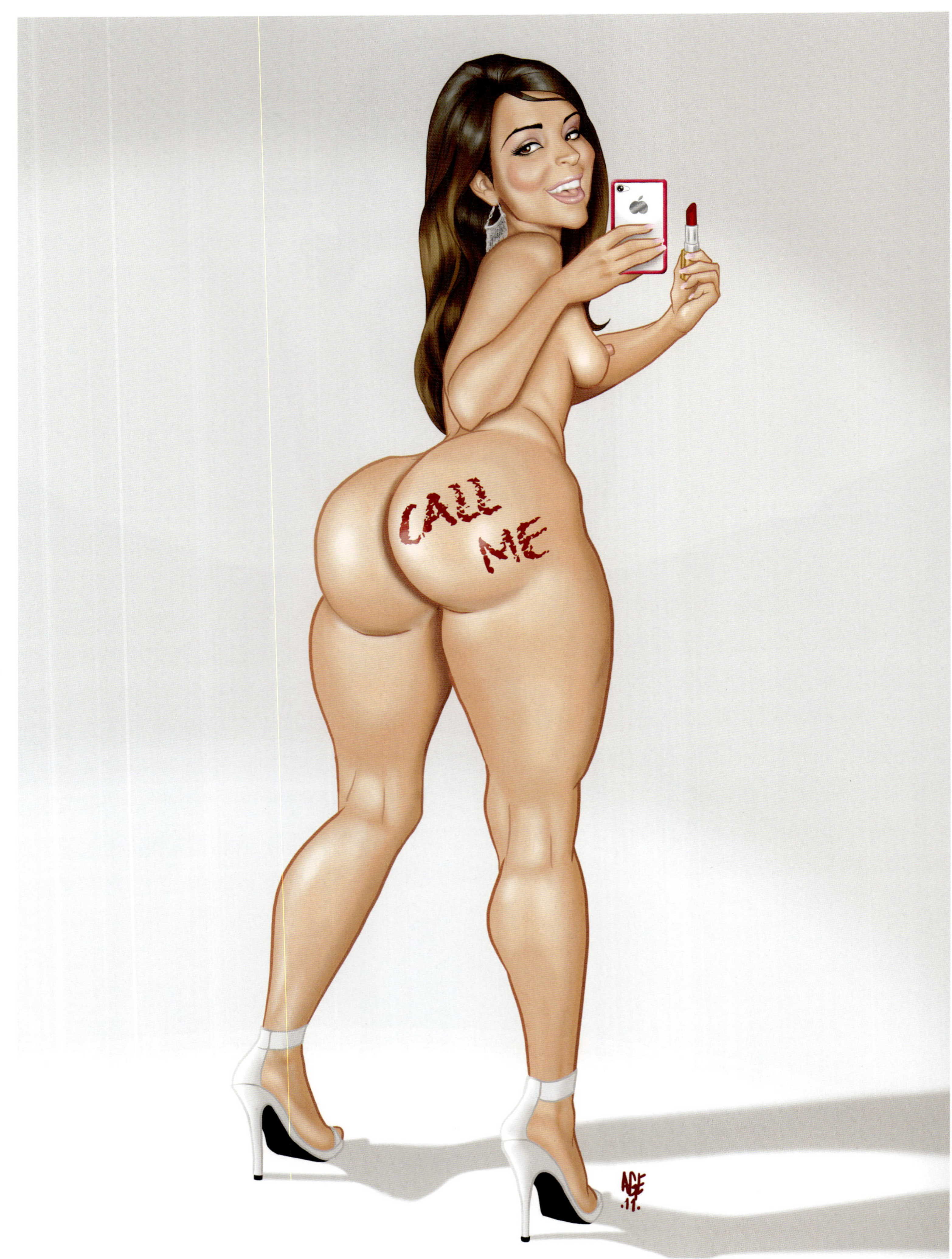

Cheeky Cell

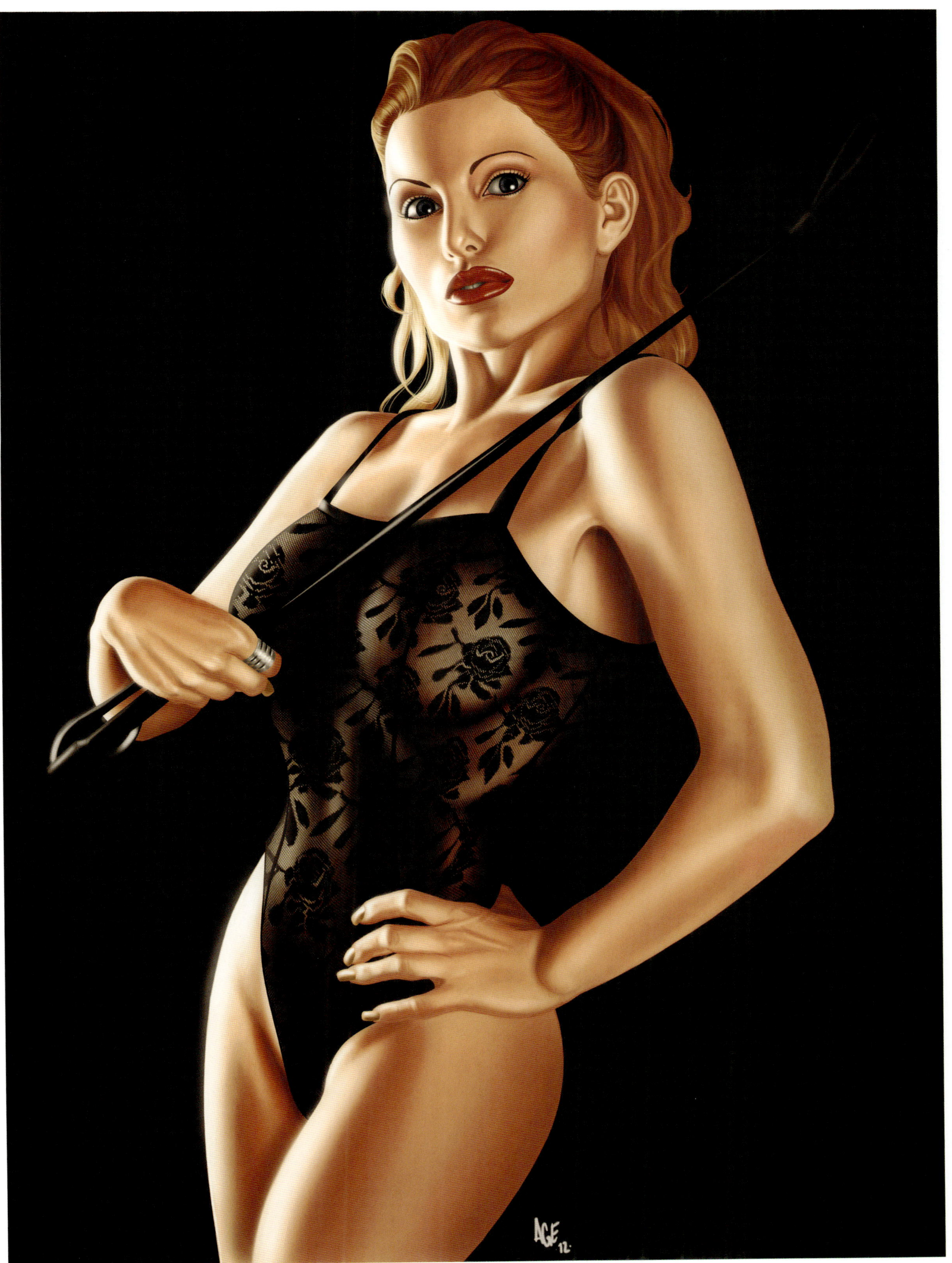

A Fresh Crop

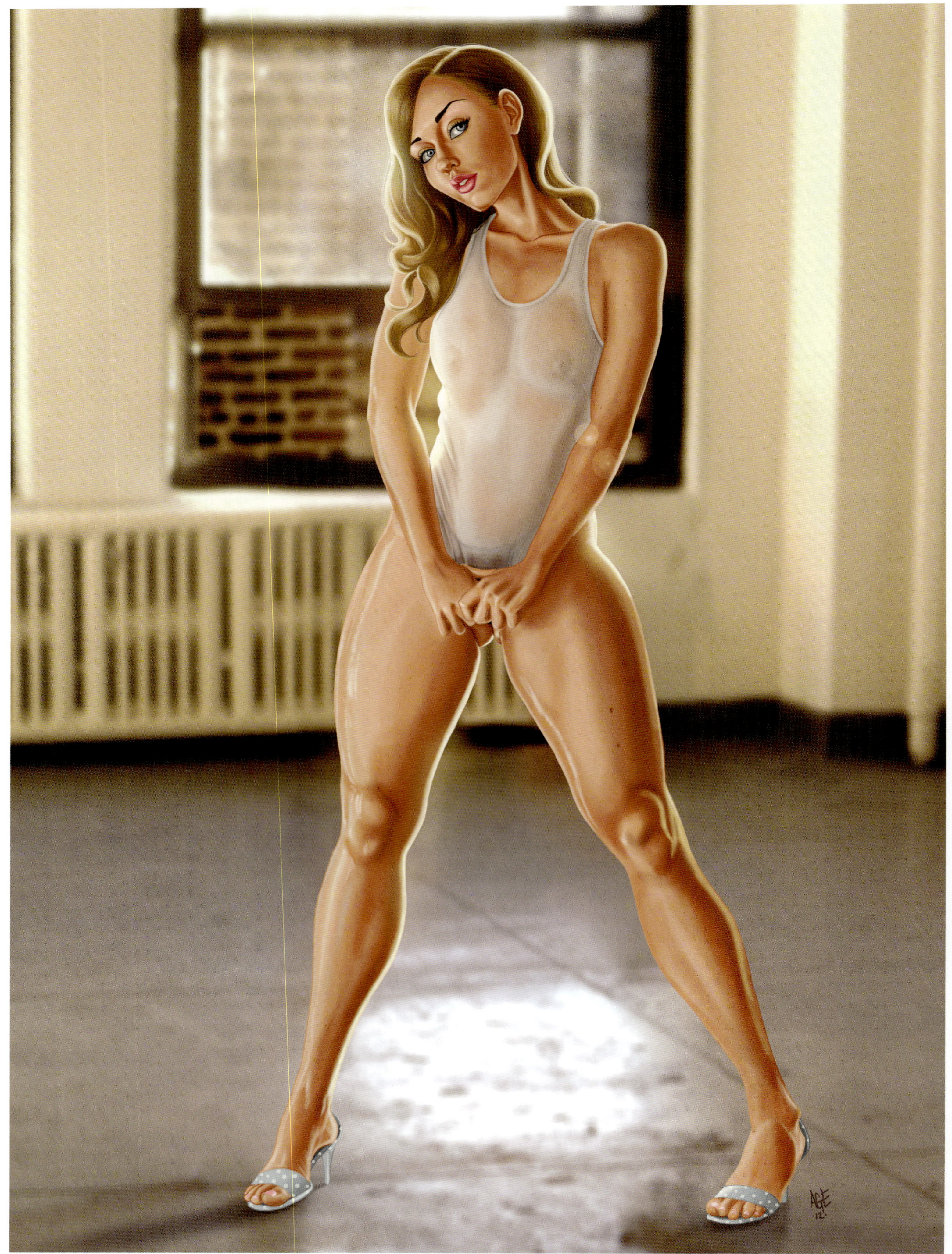

Tee-Shirt Shower

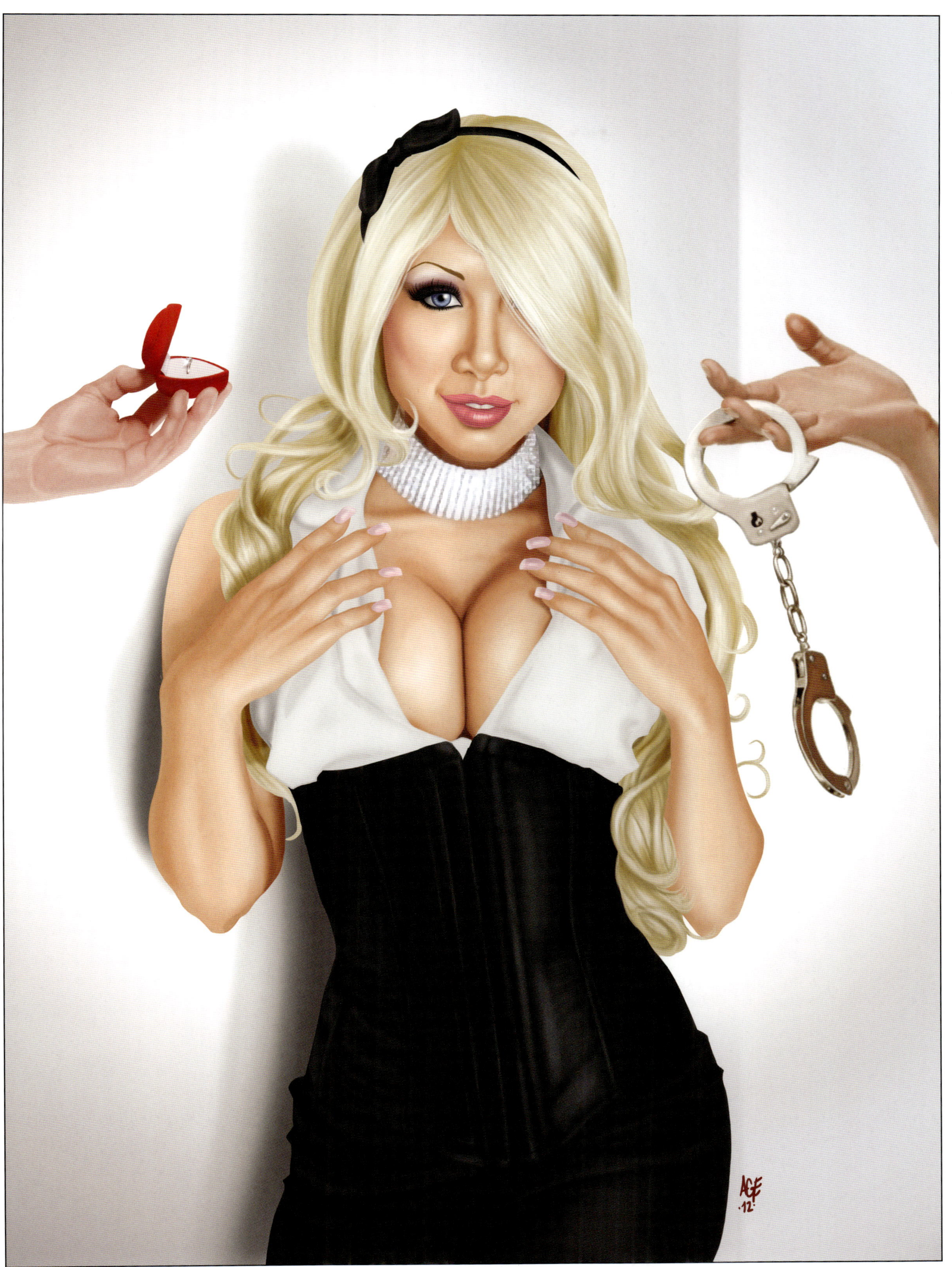

Decisions, Decisions

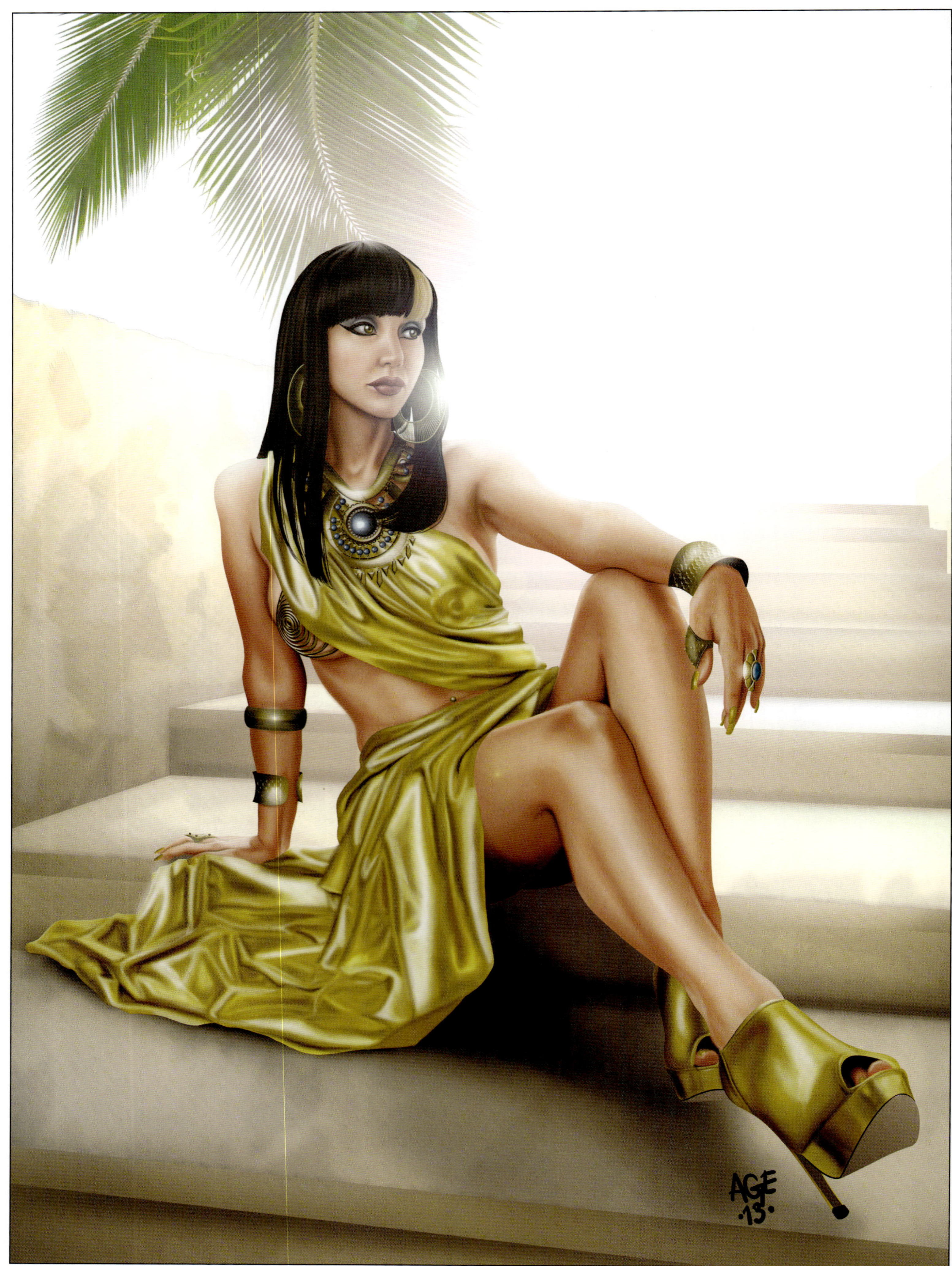

Goddess

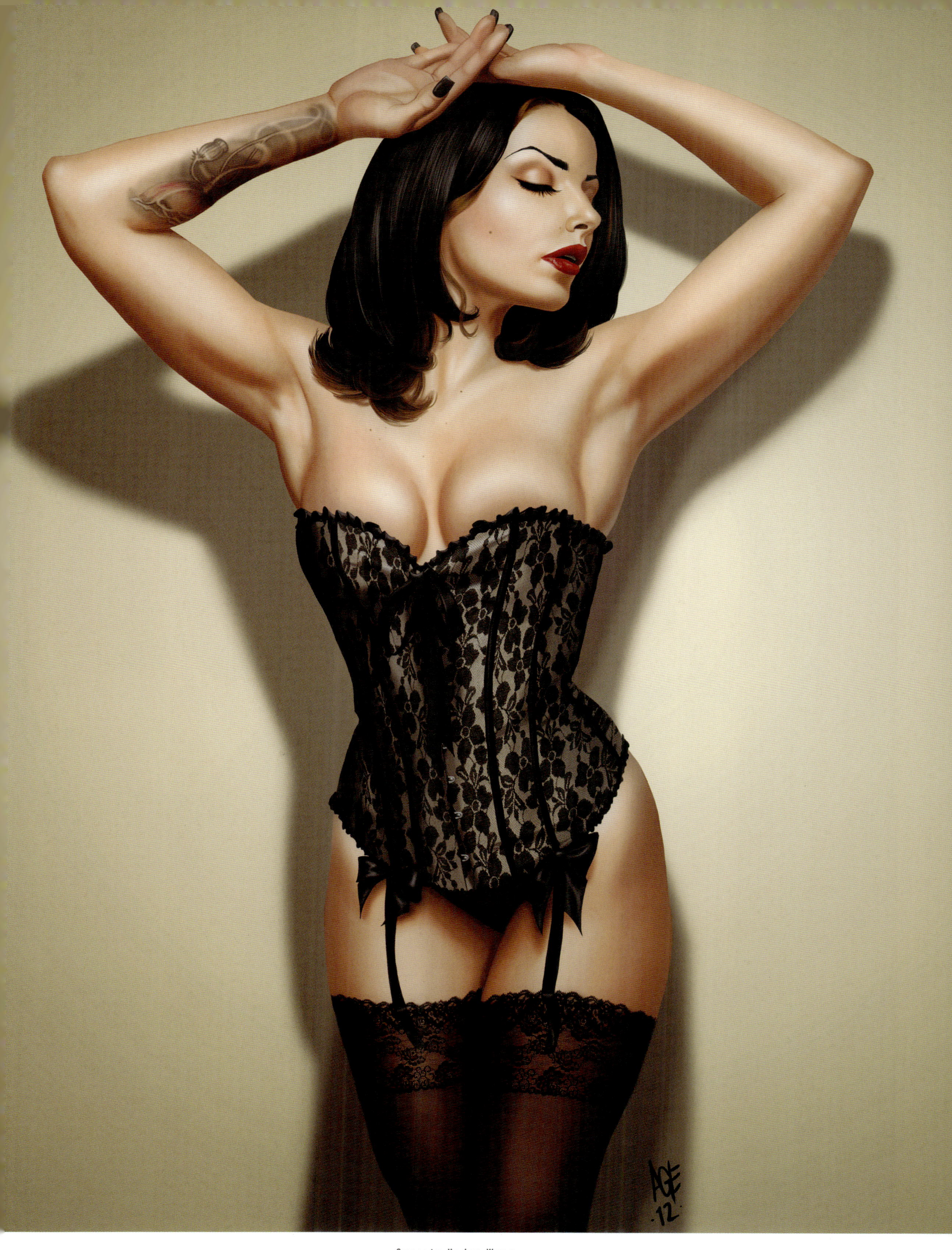

Secrets Under Wrap

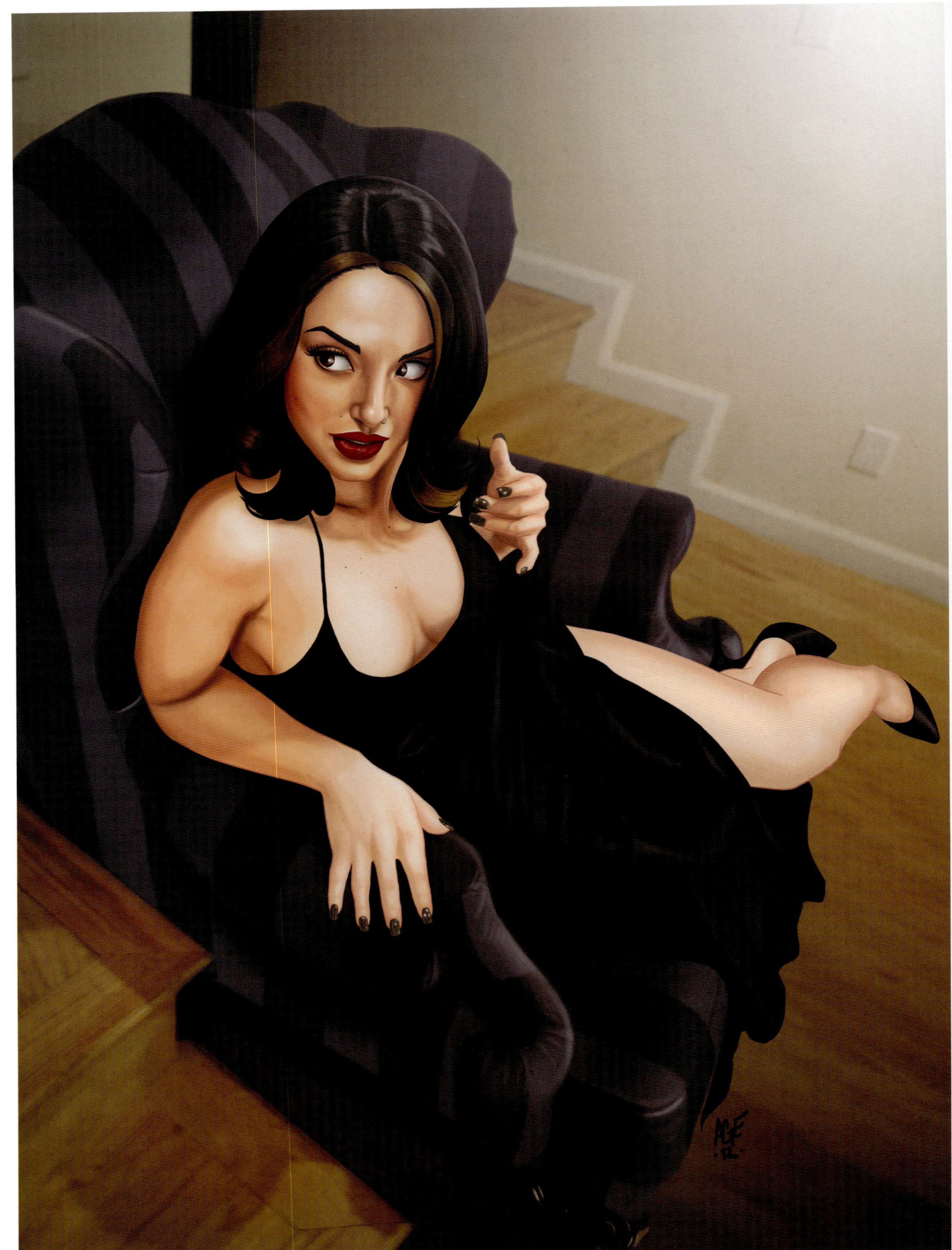

Opportunity

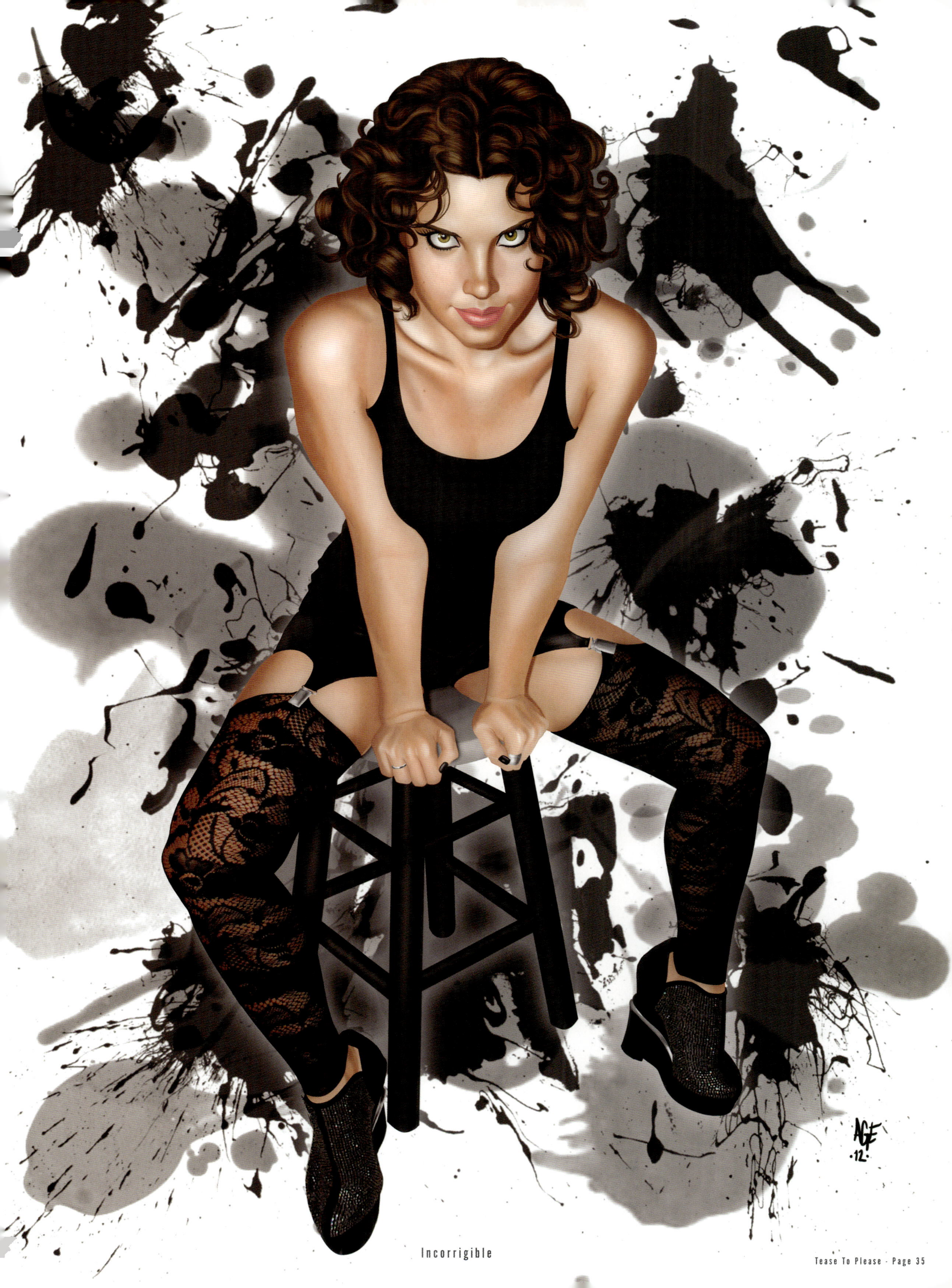

Incorrigible

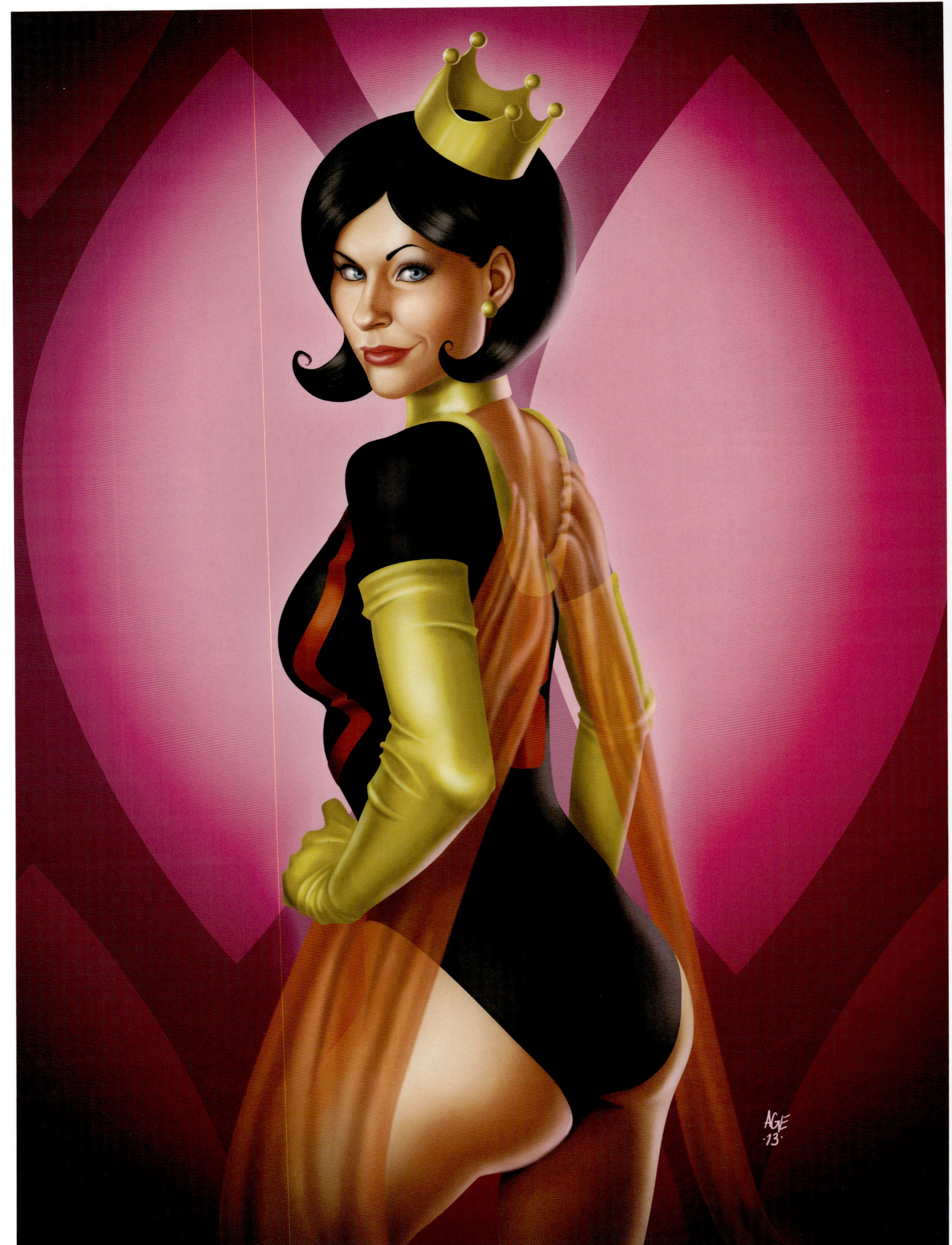

Sheila

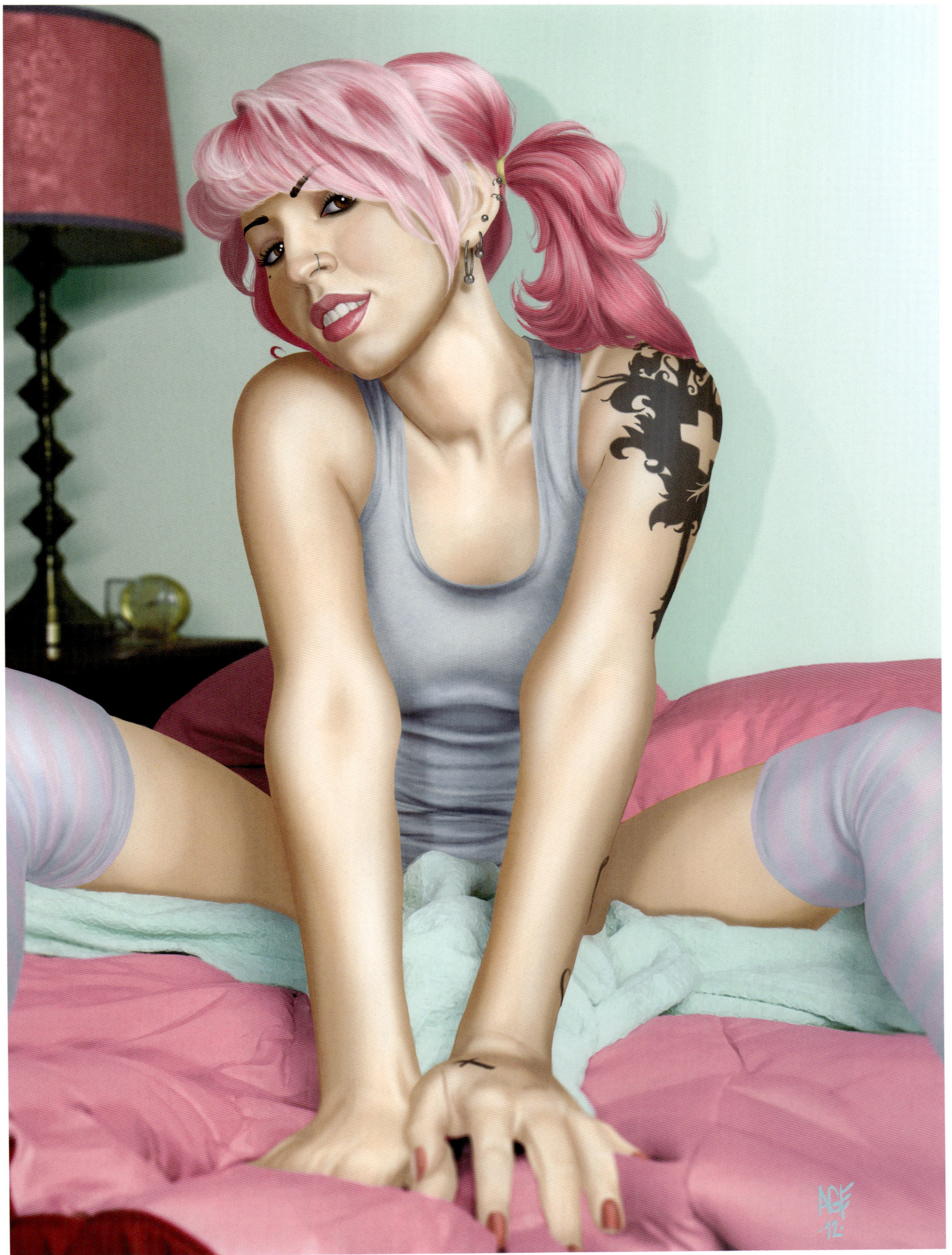

Sleepover

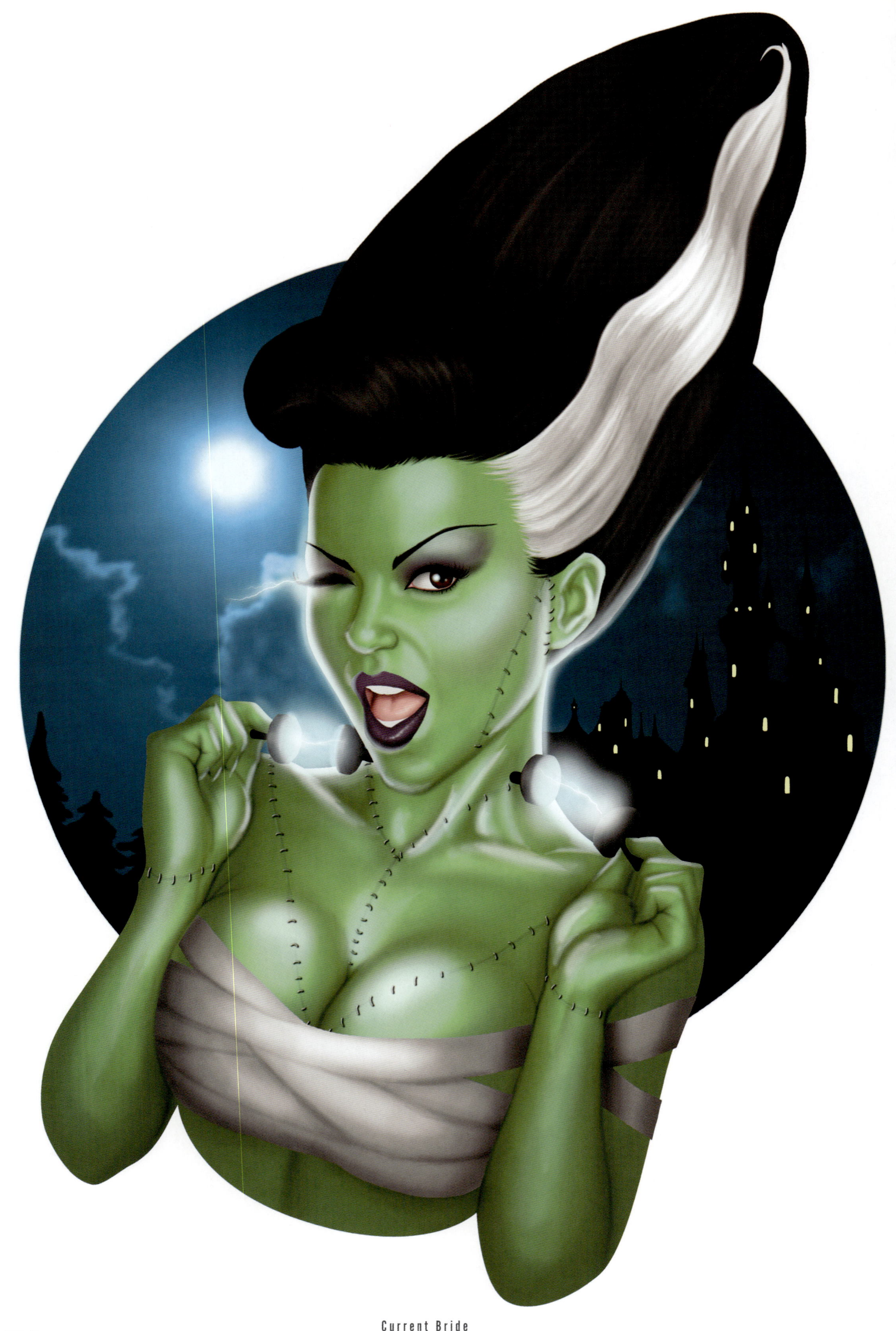

Current Bride

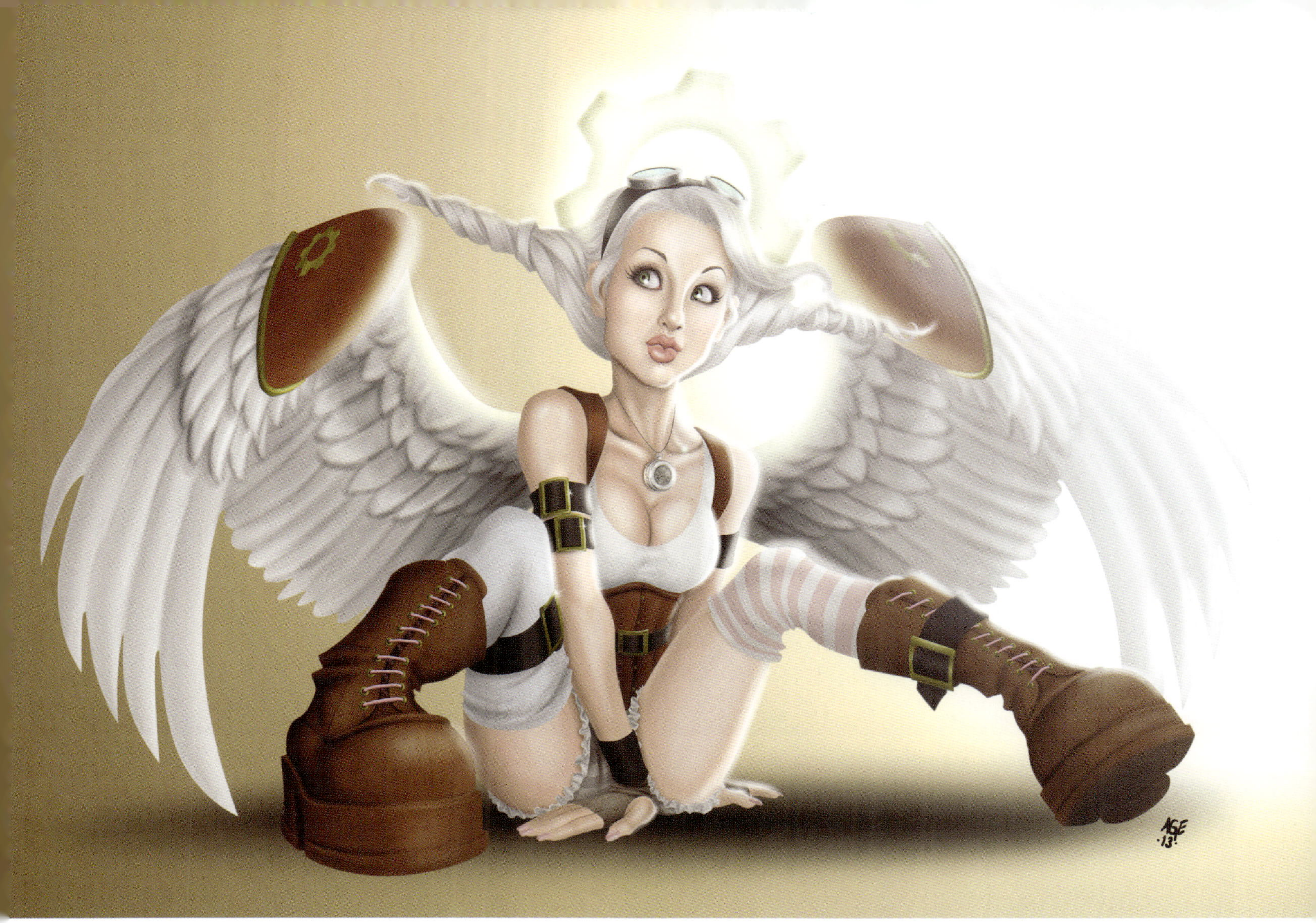

Steampunk Angel

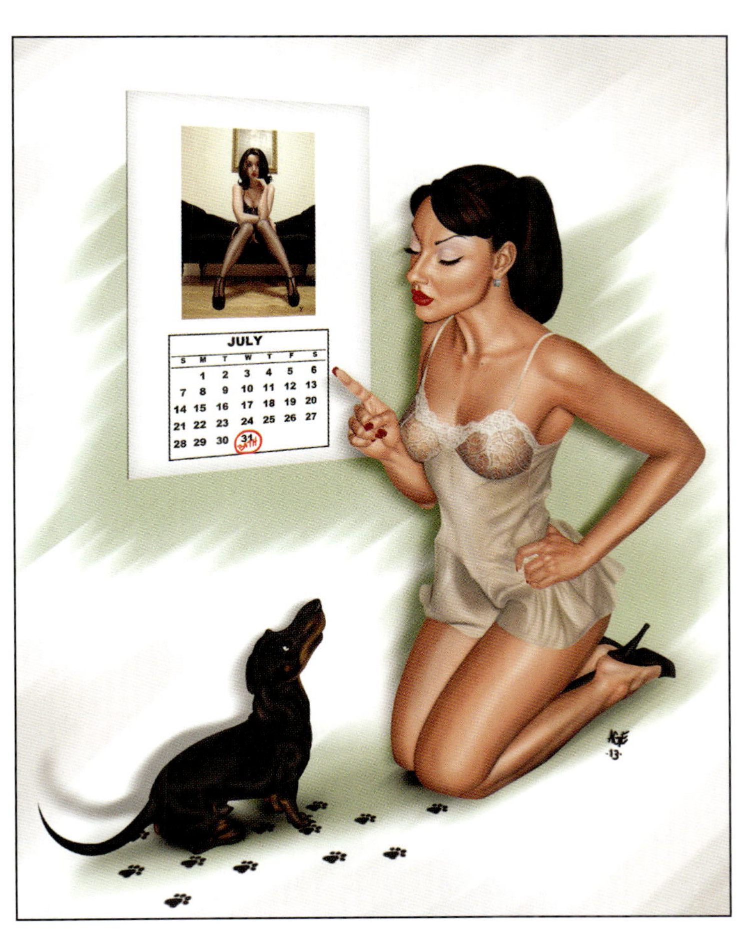

Dirty Loki

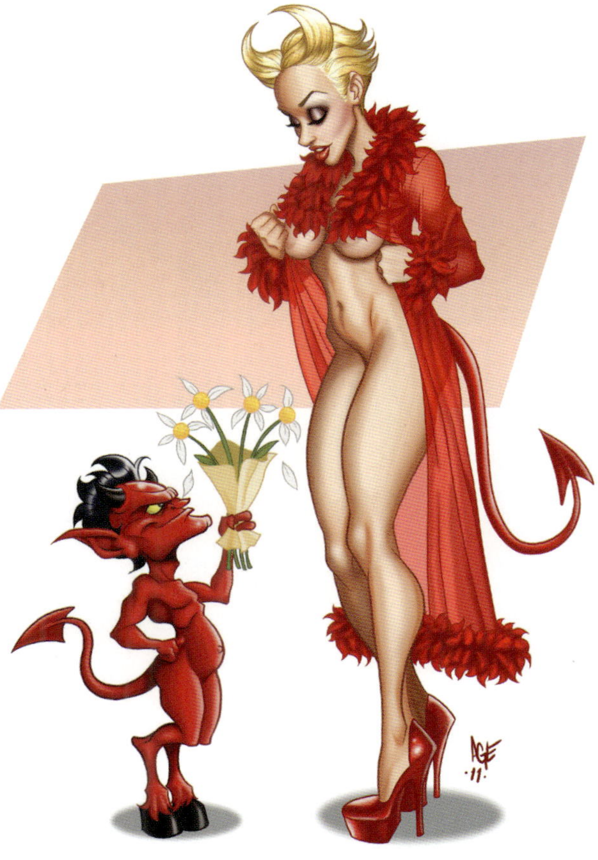

Devilish Intents

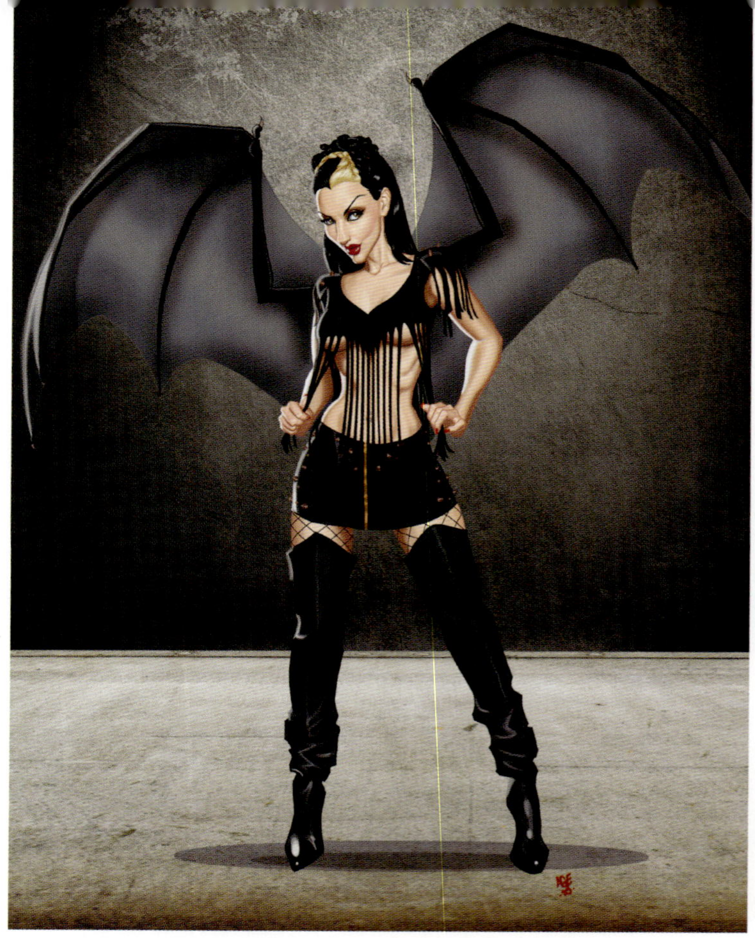

Wicked & Winged

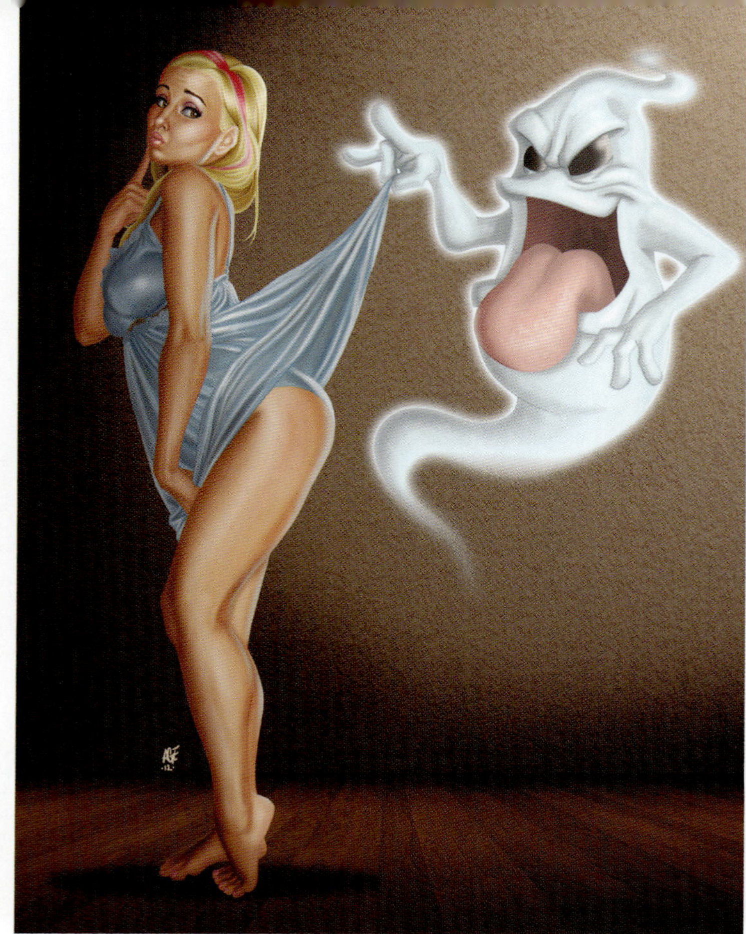

Who You Gonna Call?

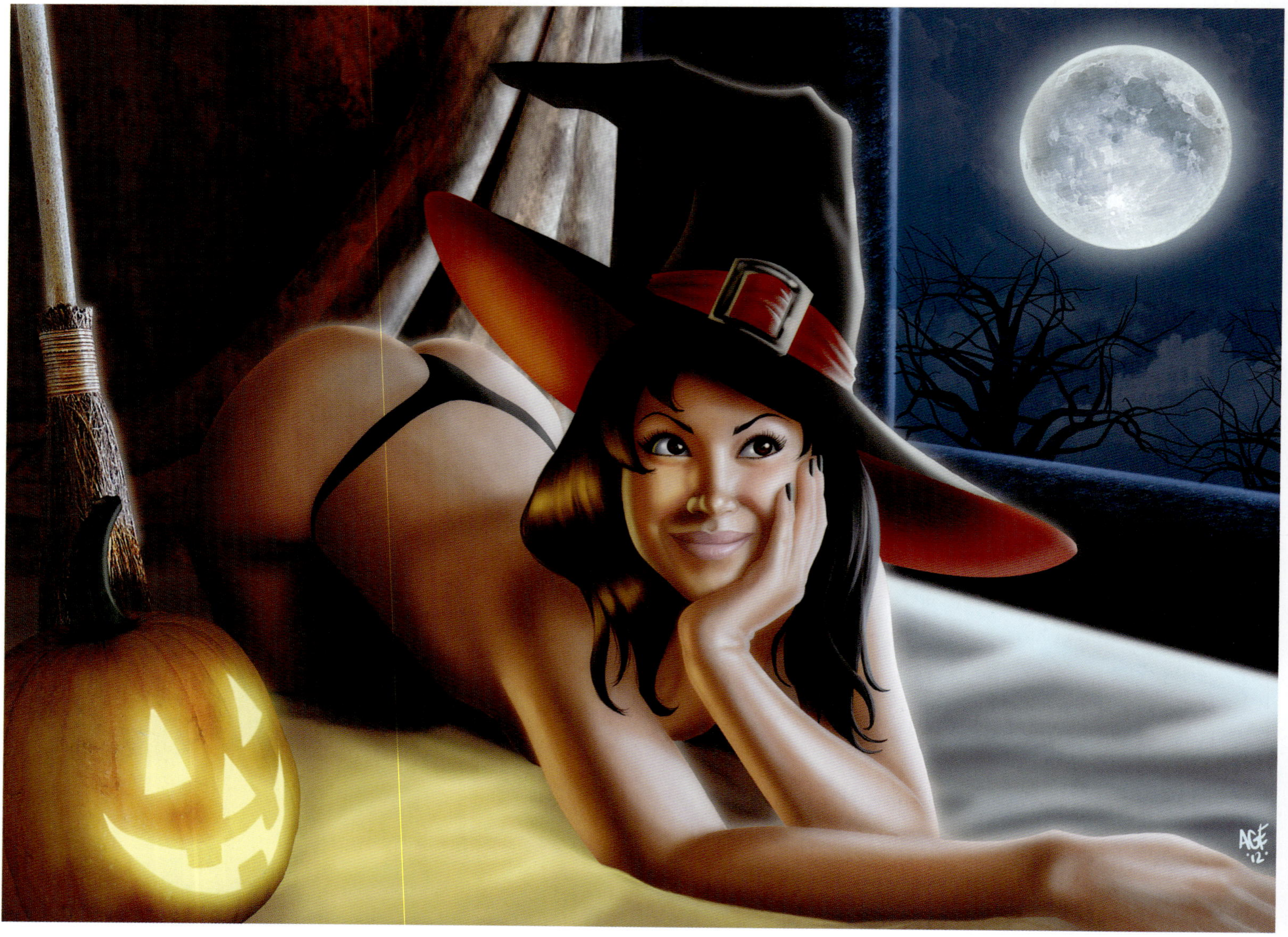

Witching Hour

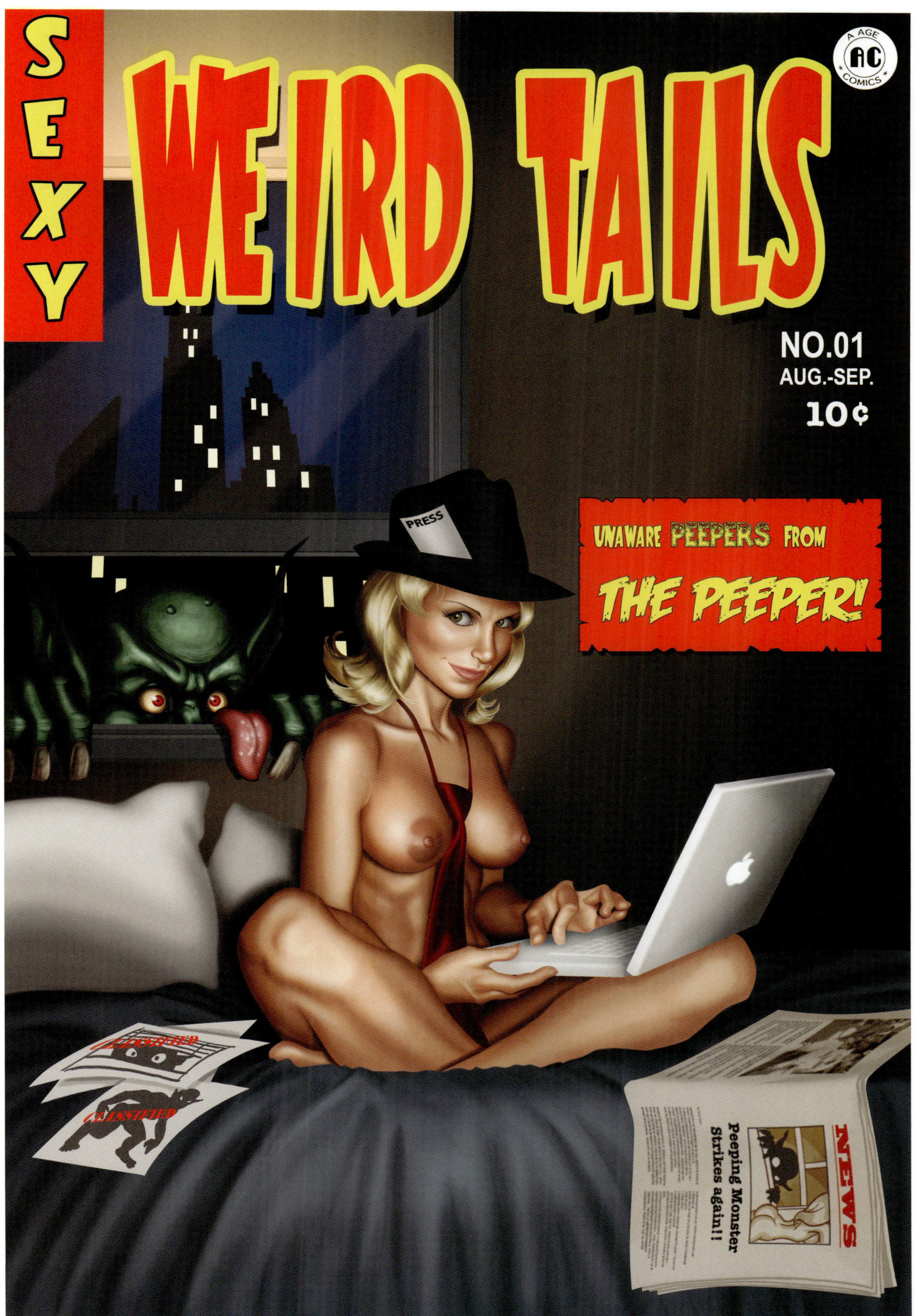

The Peeper Peeps!

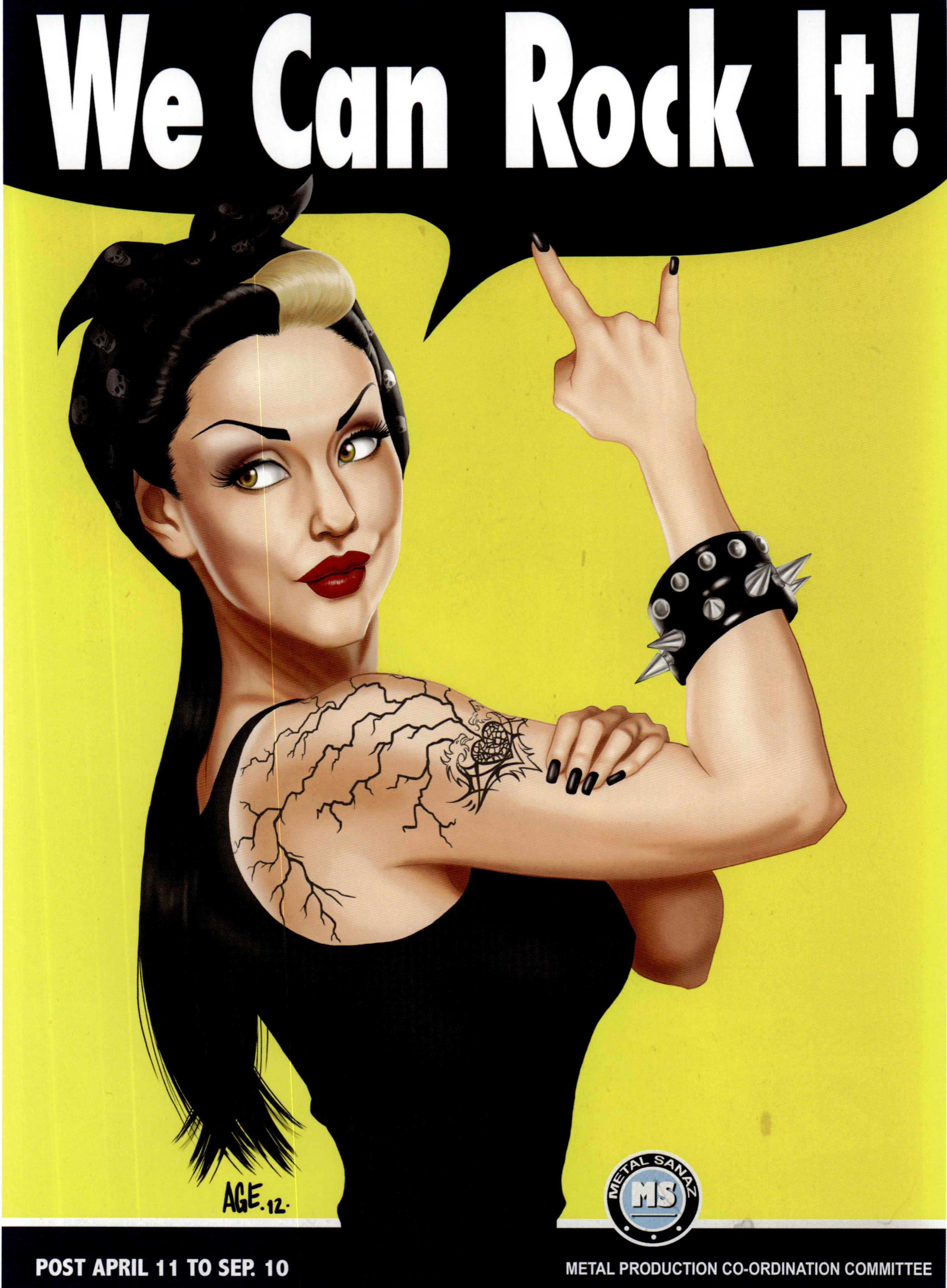

Rosie Revisited

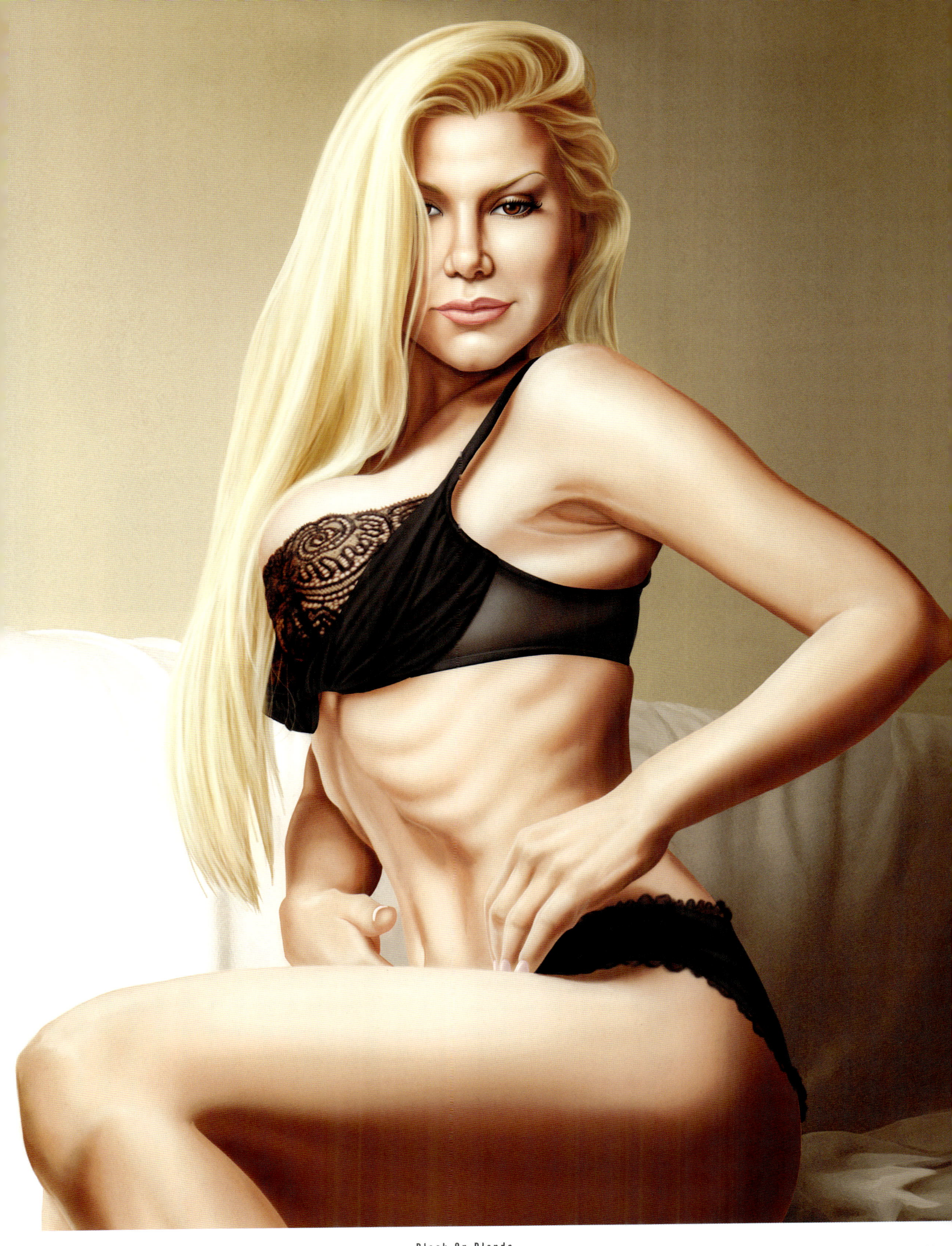

Black On Blonde

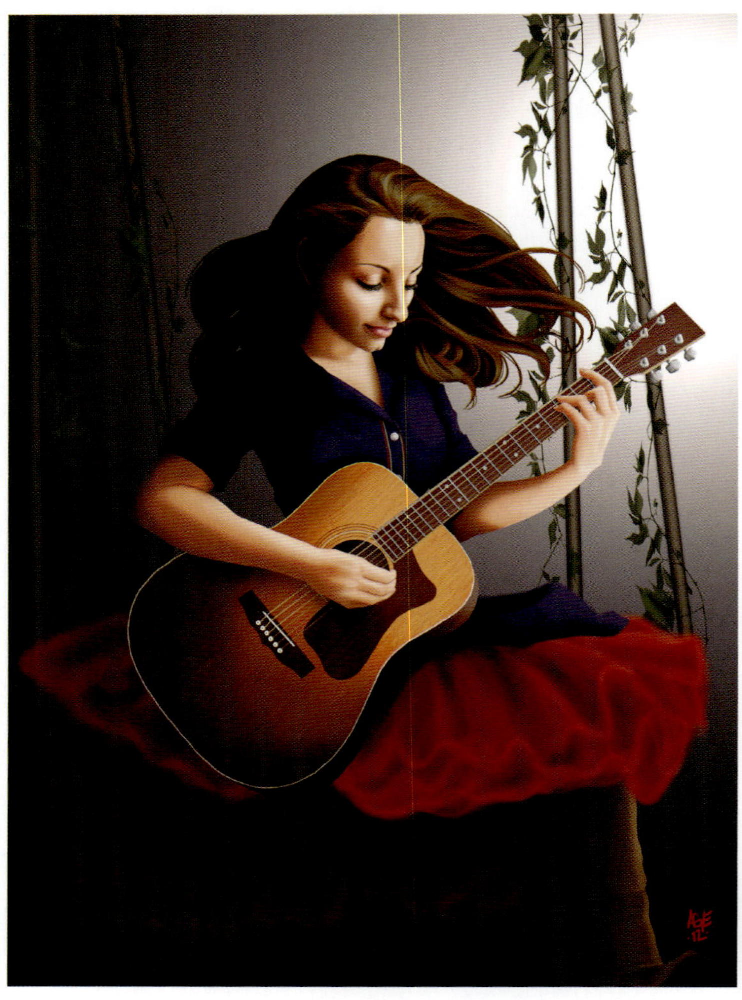

Interlude

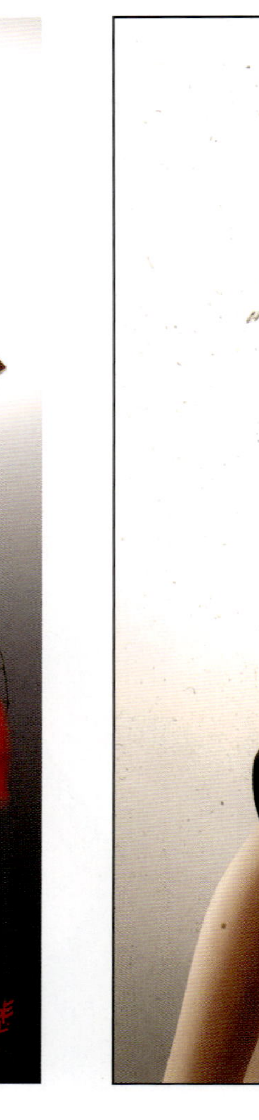

Dream a Little Dream

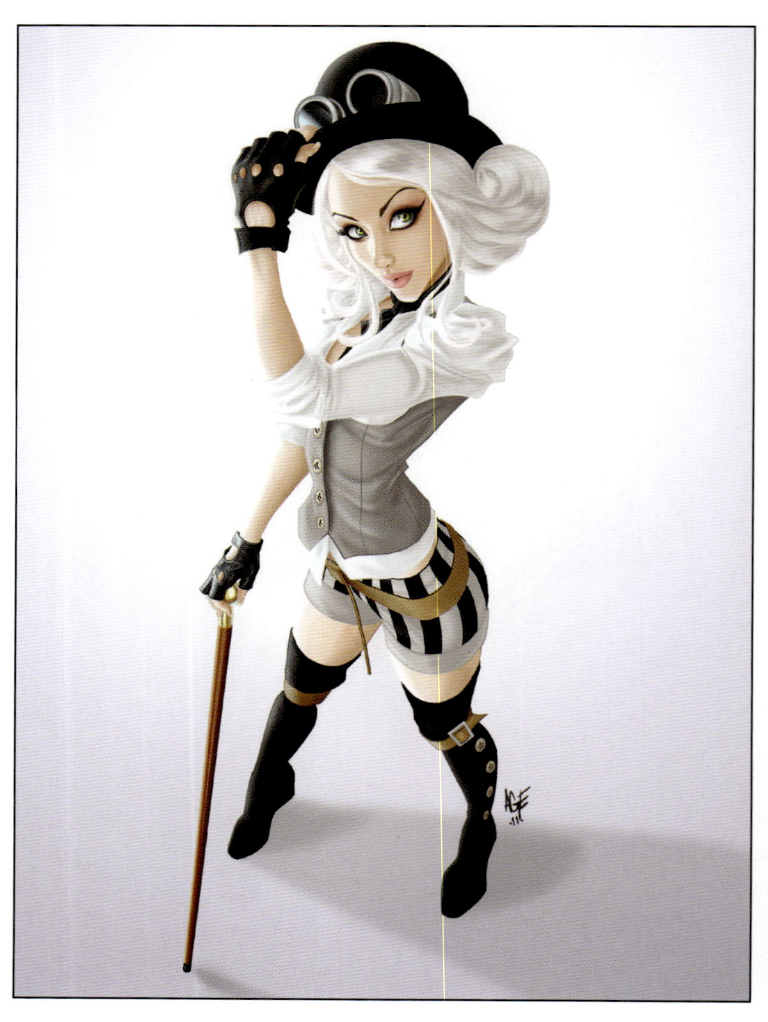

Steampunk Chic

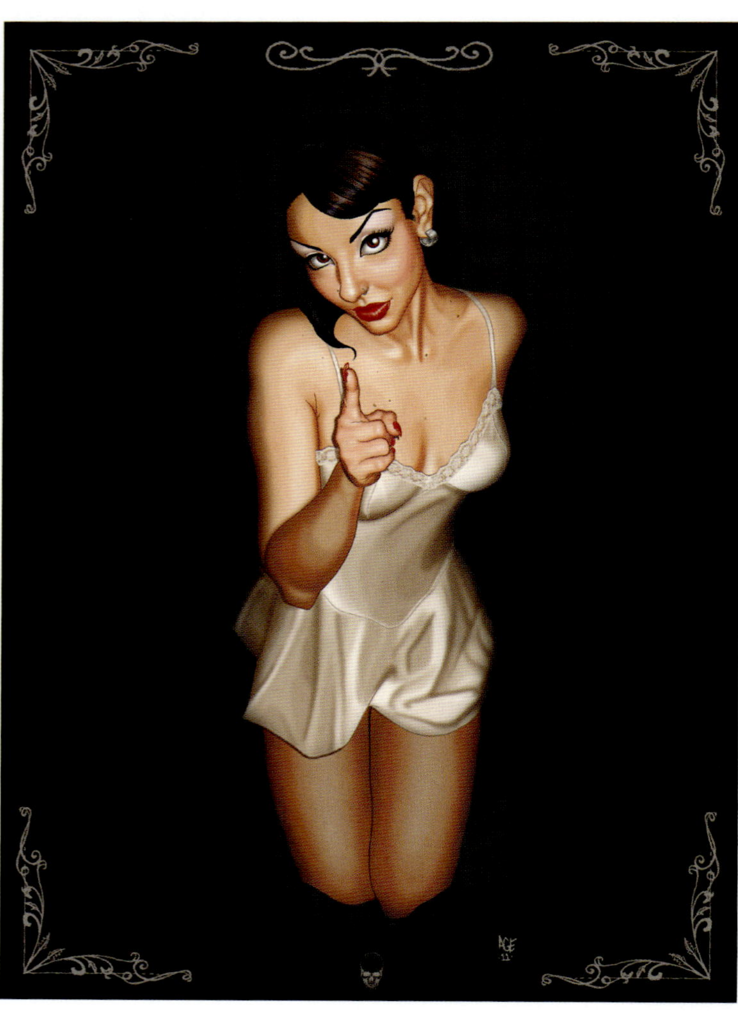

Final Warning

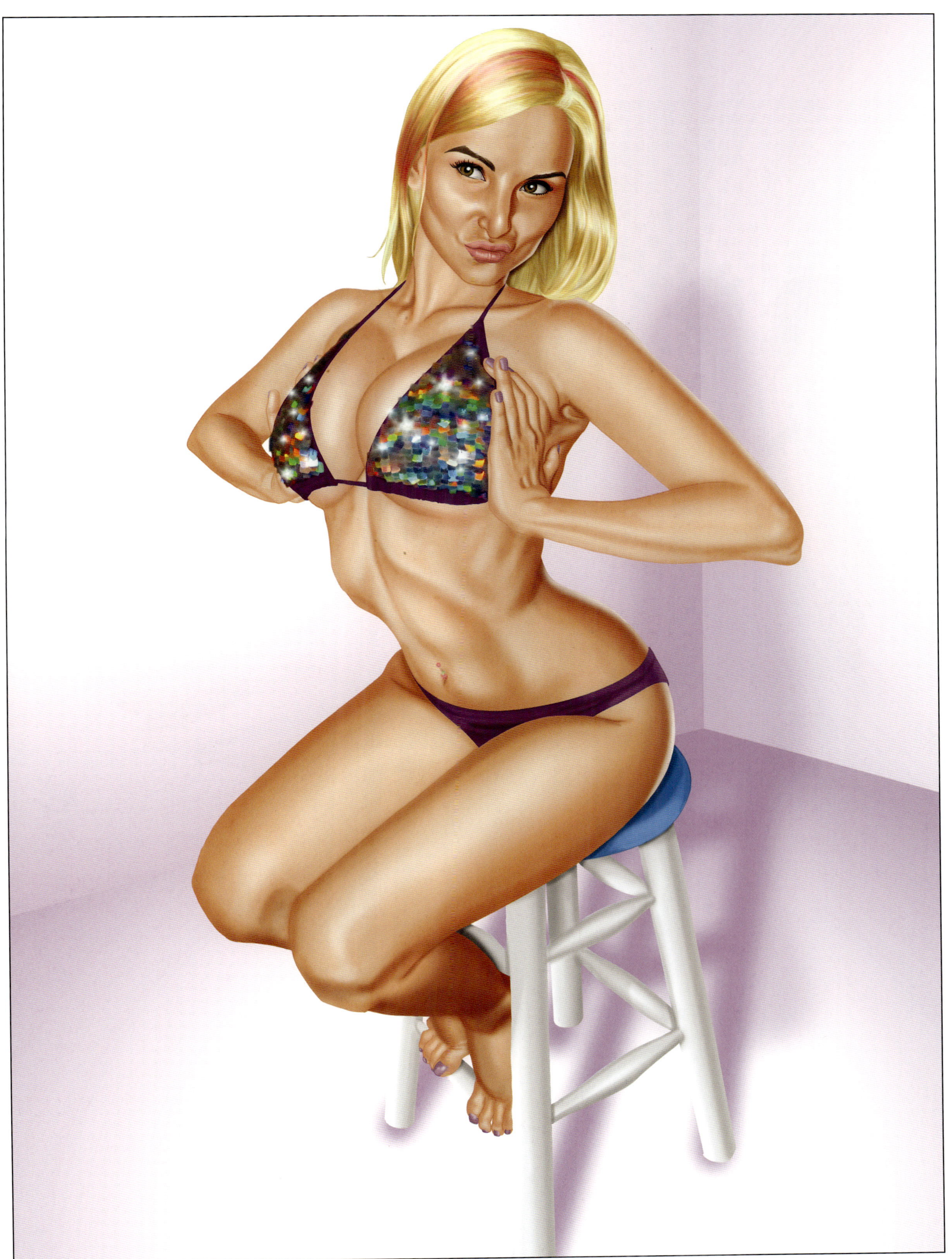

Please Adjust Your Set

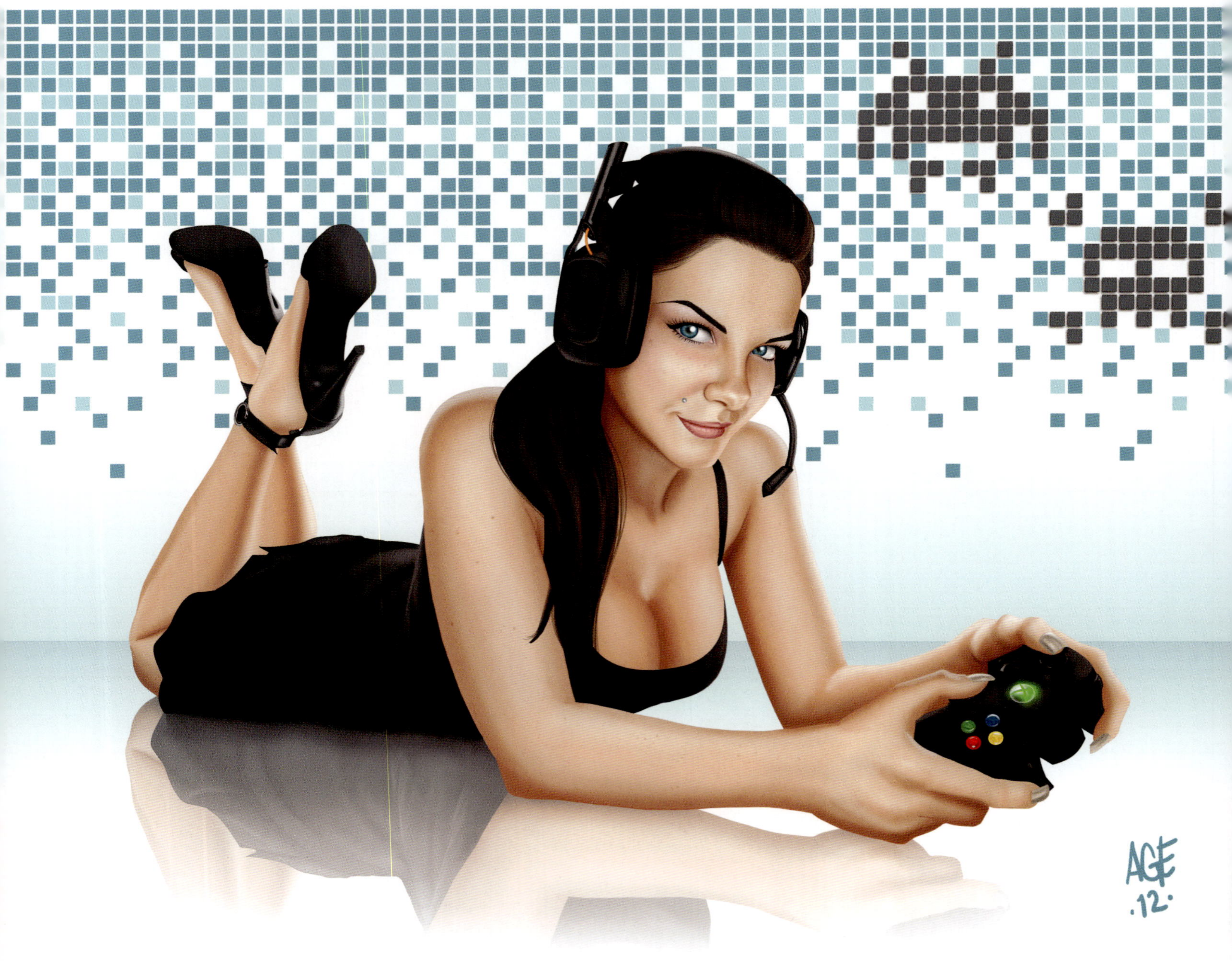

Gamer

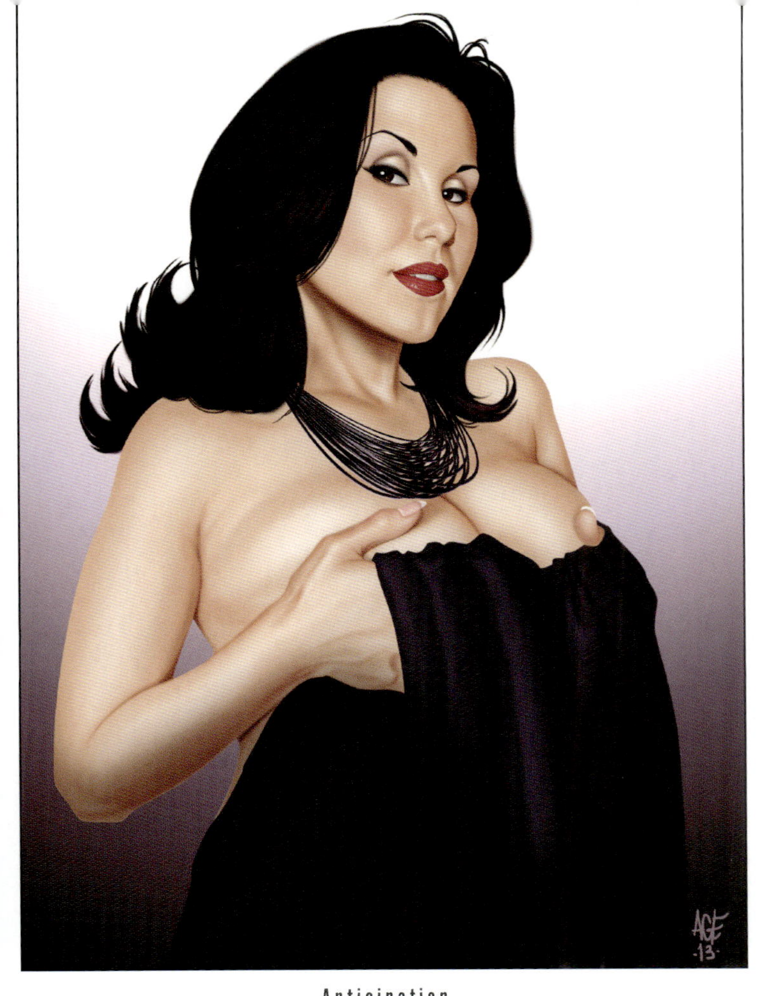

Anticipation

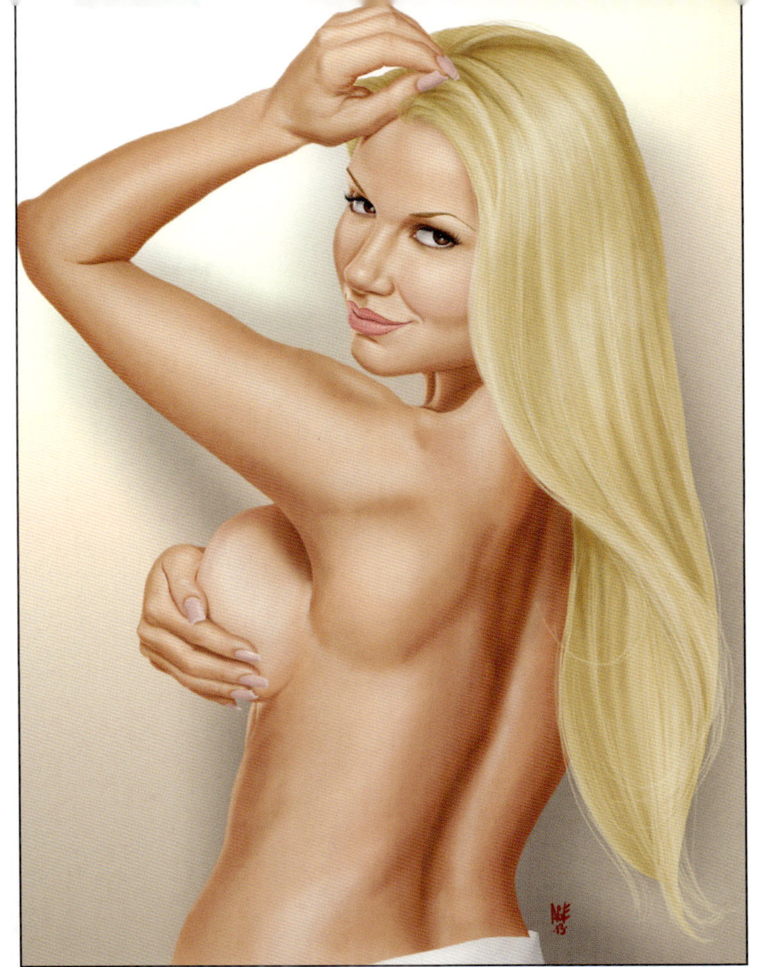

Quite the Handful

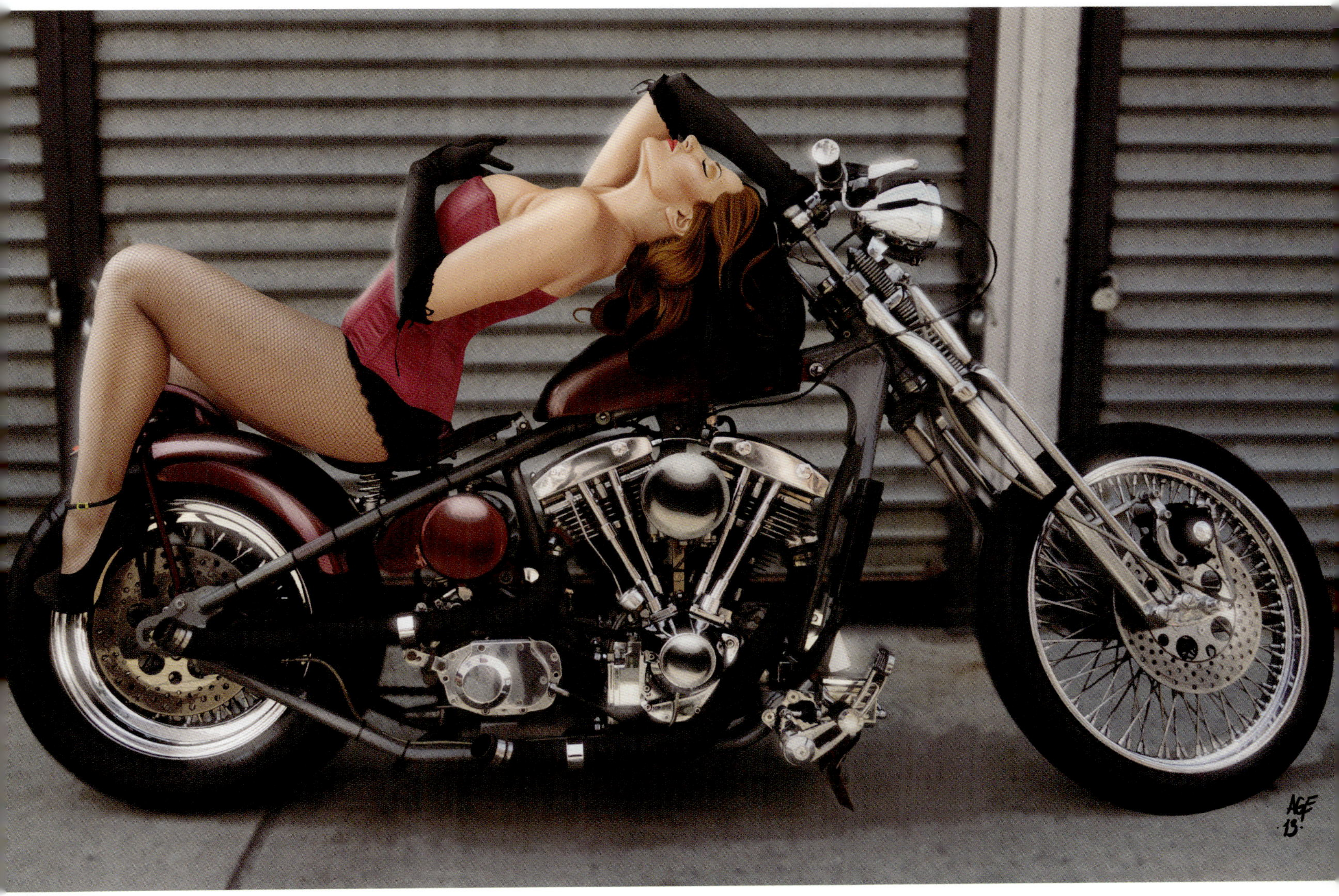

Revved Up

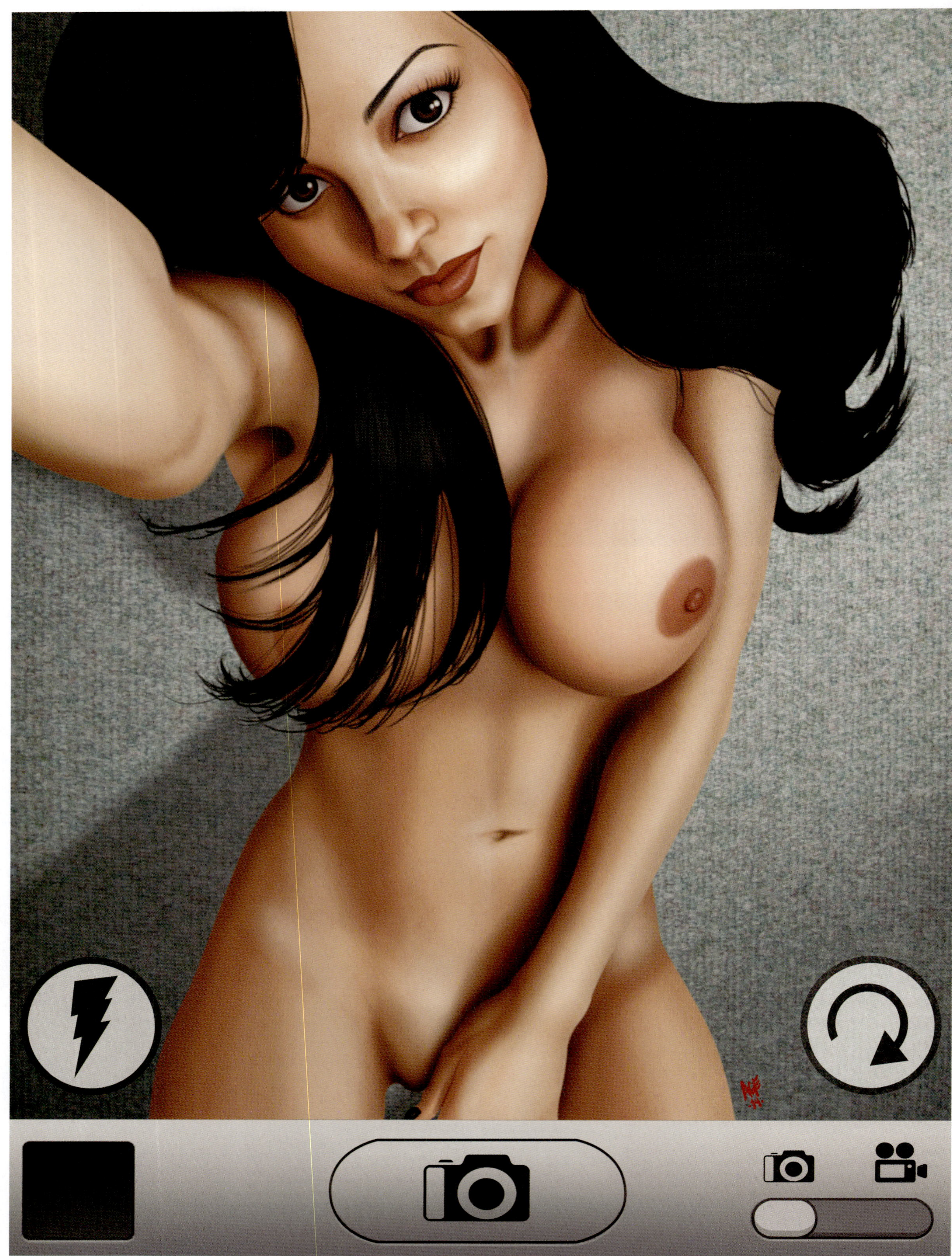

Scandalous Selfie